D0235717

OPEN
HOUSE
LONDON

OPEN HOUSE LONDON

An Exclusive Insight into 100 Architecturally Inspiring Buildings in London

Victoria Thornton

10 9 8 7 6 5 4 3 2 1

Published in 2012 by Ebury Press, an imprint of Ebury Publishing

A Random House Group Company

The Random House Group Limited Reg. No. 954009

Addresses for companies within the Random House Group can be found at www.randomhouse.co.uk

A CIP catalogue record for this book is available from the British Library

MIX
Paper from
responsible sources
FSC® C008047
FSC
www.fsc.org

The Random House Group Limited supports The Forest Stewardship Council® (FSC®), the leading international forest certification organisation. Our books carrying the FSC label are printed on FSC® certified paper. FSC is the only forest certification scheme endorsed by the leading environmental organisations, including Greenpeace. Our paper procurement policy can be found at www.randomhouse.co.uk/environment

To buy books by your favourite authors and register for offers, visit www.randomhouse.co.uk

Commissioning editor: Hannah Knowles
Project editor: Polly Boyd
Writer/researcher: Tamsin Pickeral
Design: David Rowley
New photography: Simon Upton

Printed and bound in China by C&C Offset Printin

ISBN 9780091943622

'To everyone who has been involved in Open House London'

Contents

GOOD ARCHITECTURE has a huge role to play in altering our mood. When we call an object or a building beautiful, really what we're saying is that we like the way of life it's suggesting to us. It has an attitude we're attracted to: if it was magically turned into a person, we'd like who it was. It would be convenient if we could remain in much the same mood wherever we happened to be, in a workhouse or a palace (think of how much money we'd save on redecoration), but unfortunately we're highly vulnerable to the coded messages that emanate from our surroundings. This helps to explain our passionate feelings towards architecture: it helps to decide who we are and what we feel able to do within it.

This book is full of examples of buildings that have taken the inner needs of their end users seriously. Beauty is no longer a luxury, it has been recognised as a precondition of health, flourishing and yes, sometimes, profit too. Of course, architecture can't on its own always make us into contented people. Witness the dissatisfactions that can unfold even in idyllic surroundings. One might say that architecture suggests a mood to us, which we may be too internally troubled to be able to take up. Its effectiveness could be compared to the weather: a fine day can substantially change our state of mind – and people may be willing to make great sacrifices to be nearer a sunny climate. Then again, under the weight of sufficient problems (romantic or professional confusions, for example), no amount of blue sky, and not even the greatest building, will be able to make us smile. Hence the difficulty of trying to raise architecture into a political priority: it has none of the unambiguous advantages of clean drinking water or a safe food supply.

And yet it remains vital, as this book surely shows. Flicking through these pages, we might feel both delighted and a little depressed. Delighted that so many beautiful buildings exist, sad that much of the built environment is still substandard. The salvation of British architecture lies in raising standards of taste. If one considers how rapidly and overwhelmingly this raising of taste has been achieved in cooking, there is much to be optimistic about. Consumers have learnt to ask probing questions about salt or fat levels which it wouldn't have occurred to a previous generation to raise. With the right guidance, a similar sensitivity could rapidly be fashioned to the worst features of some of the buildings that surround us. This book will, in a modest but determined way, help to change the debate about what sort of buildings we want to live, work, play and learn in.

ALAIN DE BOTTON
London, 2012

It has been 20 years since Open-City was set up as an independent, not-for-profit architecture organisation, and since then it has gone from strength to strength. Its aim is to champion the value of well-designed places and spaces in making a liveable and vibrant city, and the role everyone plays within it.

The organisation occupies a unique space in the cultural life of London, at the convergence of people, places and architectural practice. Its best-known initiative is the Open House London annual event, with which the organisation began in 1992 and which is now one of the eagerly anticipated highlights of London's cultural calendar.

Every September this event gives everyone the opportunity to get out and under the skin of some of London's most architecturally inspiring buildings, many of which are not normally open to the public, and discover for themselves how good design plays a vital role in creating and sustaining a 'liveable' city.

The early 1990s was a difficult time for architects, not least because of the economic recession at that time. Compounding this was the fact that contemporary design was not as highly valued as historic buildings: there was no government department to represent architecture, only a Department for National Heritage. In addition, there was no tradition of public engagement around architecture, even though the built environment affects everyone on a daily basis at a fundamental level. As architecture was not part of the formal education system in the UK, many people were unsure about what architects were seeking to achieve, as they often lacked the language to express their ideas, needs and aspirations for the quality of the buildings and public spaces around them. By offering an opportunity to experience great places and spaces at first hand, Open House London aims to generate an informal but deeper understanding of the impact that these can have on the individual.

Attitudes have changed since then: the Department of Culture, Media and Sport has a minister for architecture, while the research that we do via Open House London every year shows that an ever-increasing number of Londoners think that contemporary architecture makes a positive contribution to the capital.

The Open House London annual event

About 100 people attended the first Open House London event in 1992 – a figure that by 2011 grew to an astonishing 250,000. At the heart of the event remains a simple but incredibly powerful concept: showcasing outstanding architecture for all to experience, completely for free.

By 1994, 200 contemporary and historic buildings across London featured in the event. The number of buildings, walks, talks and tours in the event grew, by 2011, to more than 700, across almost all of London's boroughs. The aim has always been to open eyes and minds to unfamiliar – and sometimes challenging – design by offering an opportunity to experience it at first hand. Perhaps most importantly, Open House London gives people an opportunity to look afresh, and reflect on, their own neighbourhood, or to discover the architecture of a new area of the capital that might be less familiar to them.

In 1997, Open House Junior was created – an extensive series of creative, architecture-related activities for children and their families and friends, designed to engage young minds as 'architectives' discovering the built world around them. By the 20th anniversary celebrations in 2012, this had emerged as a standalone festival on the theme of the 'child-friendly city'. Most recently, the Open House concept has spread internationally, and is now being replicated across Europe, the United States and the Far East, with the Open House family of cities attracting a total of 1 million participants globally every year.

The choice of buildings

Much of the success of Open House London lies in the enormous diversity of buildings featured. While small private houses attract great interest, Open House London encompasses all types of building from key government departments, contemporary workplaces, schools, health centres, sports facilities, cultural institutions and other community buildings.

It is this diversity that has influenced the selection of buildings in this book. Although some famous London landmarks are included, Open House London mainly showcases the perhaps lesser-known and smaller projects that form a vital part of the London landscape that we see, use and experience every day. Some are featured because they provide an outstanding example of a particular architect's work, others because they illustrate how historic buildings can be adapted creatively for new uses, or have played a vital role in regenerating a wider area. Yet quality remains the standard for inclusion: any building featured must represent a successful design solution to a set of issues, circumstances or particular challenges, in order to show the 'art of the possible'.

The value of good architecture cannot be underestimated. Buildings matter, and they significantly affect the way people feel about their day-to-day lives. We hope that this book will illustrate how well-designed buildings and spaces can play a major role in making London such a great city, and that it will inspire you to take a second look at the buildings around you.

Most importantly, we would like to thank all the featured buildings' owners, managers and other personnel, all of whom have opened their doors to engage the community through Open House London over the years – and especially all of those who have offered help and input for this book. Without their incredibly generous support, effort and goodwill neither the event nor the book would be possible.

Victoria Thornton

Amnesty International UK Headquarters
Angel Building
30 St Mary Axe
Chiswick Business Park
Economist Building
Lloyd's of London
Gibbs Building, Wellcome Trust
Former London Underground Head Office, 55 Broadway
Congress House
Imagination
10 Queen Street Place
120 Fleet Street, *former* Daily Express *building*
City Gate House & 50 Finsbury Square
BT Tower
Channel 4 Television
BBC Broadcasting House
Abbey Mills Pumping Station
Crossness Engines House
Trinity Buoy Wharf Container City

LONDON AT WORK

'If London is to remain a relevant player in world culture and finance, excellence in architecture must be supported. Responding to environmental concerns, and proving old and new can comfortably co-exist in remodelled spaces, are some of the positive effects.'
Open House London visitor

As one of the world's great cities, and a major global centre for international business and finance, London sustains an almost infinite range of businesses, all reflected in the diversity of its workspace and office design. The nature of work has, of course, changed greatly since the 19th and early 20th centuries, when heavy industry and manufacturing drove the economy, however many fine industrial buildings and examples of infrastructure, such as Crossness Engines House, remain as reminders of the Victorian and early modern industrial landscape.

Yet increasingly, London's built environment, and indeed the skyline that symbolises it around the world, has been dominated over the past 30 years by the new office and commercial buildings at the heart of the City of London, such as Lloyd's of London and 30 St Mary Axe. Generating vigorous debate then and now, such tall buildings have transformed London's skyline, and continue to do so with the addition of new towers such as the Heron Tower and the Shard London Bridge. London has also seen the emergence of new business districts, such as Canary Wharf, which regenerated the former docklands that fell into decline in the 1970s and 1980s. Here, in the east, creative industries have also inhabited and transformed the once-derelict landscape: at Trinity Buoy Wharf Container City, for example, industrial units such as shipping containers have been put to new uses to create adaptable, reusable and low-cost live/work spaces more suitable to the needs of artists, designers and small businesses.

Today, most of the workforce is engaged in knowledge-based or service industries: it is well known that there is a direct link between well-designed offices and productivity, and that businesses that provide a positive, well-designed environment are more likely to attract better employees, and keep them for longer. Yet workspace design also influences – and is influenced by – how the business is perceived by clients and customers, how it responds to continuous technological innovation, and how it relates to the wider environment, physically, socially and economically.

Generally, it is London's new office buildings and skyscrapers that have attracted the most attention. However, perhaps one of the most distinctive trends over the past two decades is the remodelling of older buildings (not just 'historic' – even those from the 1980s) to create flexible, sustainable and inspirational workspaces suitable for the 21st century. City Gate House and 50 Finsbury Square, 10 Queen Street Place, Imagination, the Angel Building and Amnesty International UK Headquarters are among the many imaginative, high-quality examples of reuse across the capital. Increasingly, also, there is a mix of uses – retail, residential and leisure facilities; these, combined with high-quality landscaping and public art, can help to create distinctive and successful places that can act as catalysts for wider regeneration. This concern with social and economic, as well as environmental, sustainability, is likely to become ever more important in the coming decades as London's workforce expands and becomes ever more diverse.

Amnesty International UK Headquarters, EC2

I n 2003, Witherford Watson Mann and Gregori Chiarotti won a competition to design the new Amnesty International UK Headquarters. The organisation required a building that would serve a number of different purposes: namely, to bring all the staff and volunteers together to work under one roof to encourage closer working, to provide room for training and meetings, and to create stimulating and inspiring outreach facilities, including an auditorium, and education and exhibition space for the public to visit. The design required a particularly sensitive approach: it had to accommodate these specific criteria required by the organisation while keeping costs and ostentation to a minimum, as befits a charity dedicated to campaigning for human rights. The project was completed in 2005.

Rather than designing a new build, two former furniture factories in Shoreditch,

east London, were purchased and redesigned to create a single, cohesive building. Both were four storeys high – the first was built in 1911 and the second in 1954. To unite the buildings, the architects created an adjoining atrium area, which acts as the principal artery for the traffic of staff and visitors. The stairs are open to the office floors at each level, to increase the feeling of accessibility, and two big windows provide plenty of natural light. The large, open offices provide space for between 8 and 16 people – a response to Amnesty's teamworking culture.

Close to this central thoroughfare are meeting rooms, a kitchen and a 'breakout area', while scattered throughout the building are further places designed to encourage communication, including socialising. A key space for Amnesty visitors is the Human Rights Action Centre. Housing an exhibition area, an education room and a lecture hall – located where the old factory's loading bay once was – the aim of the centre is to raise public awareness of human rights issues and to convey some of the drama and conflict involved in the campaigns. The space

allows visitors to look down into working offices on the lower-ground floor.

The exterior and interior of the Amnesty International UK Headquarters have a utilitarian feel while being modern, light and airy. The outside is blue-brown brick, with deeply recessed windows in attractive but simple hardwood frames (replacing the existing steel-frame windows), and the internal finishes are simple and robust, featuring exposed brickwork and reclaimed pitch pine floors. The building has achieved the perfect balance of being functional yet enjoyable.

Opposite: *Amnesty's headquarters are situated in what was once two factory buildings in east London, now made into a single unit by an adjoining atrium area.*
Above: *Inside the atrium extension, the main thoroughfare for staff and visitors.*

The Angel Building resulted from the reimagining of a dreary, early-1980s commercial block that was home to British Telecom for several decades. This fully refurbished and extended building has been designed to act as a catalyst for the regeneration of the area. The redevelopment was commissioned by property developers Derwent London and the architects Allford Hall Monaghan Morris undertook the work (see also pages 104, 152, 160), which was completed in 2010.

Given the prominent site at the junction of Islington High Street, St John Street and Pentonville Road, and the extensive public façades, it was important that the new office block would complement surrounding buildings. A striking exterior plus soft landscaping in a disused space in front of the building on St John's Street helped the architects to achieve their aim. A newly landscaped public realm, set around mature trees and designed by J & L Gibbons, creates a natural progression between the building and the street. A retail space and restaurant were incorporated into the street frontage. Early occupants of the building include a charity, an online travel company and a software firm.

The development of the Angel Building had two key objectives: to create a positive and inspirational working environment, and to do so in as sustainable a manner as possible. Part of the success of this building lies in the reuse of its existing concrete structure, thus eliminating the need for demolition and construction, while also cutting costs. An energy-efficient glazed skin was wrapped around the exterior, and the outdoor courtyard was incorporated into the new design to form a central atrium. At five storeys high, and with a glass roof, the atrium provides a spacious, light-filled social area at the heart of the building. There are informal seating areas throughout, with views from the higher floors down to the atrium. The internal scheme of the atrium is one of pure space and clean lines, enlivened with custom-commissioned art works. On display is a particularly interesting sculptural form (which doubles as a seat) by architect Ian McChesney – *Out of the Strong Came Forth Sweetness*, modelled on treacle dripping from an inverted spoon.

Among the defining elements of the Angel Building are the spacious roof terraces, some of which are landscaped, that afford remarkable views over the

Left: *Soft landscaping enhances the public space around the Angel Building.*
Opposite: *A bird's eye view of the central atrium and Ian McChesney's sculpture,* Out of the Strong Came Forth Sweetness.

City of London and the West End. The uppermost terrace is used for meetings and events, while the others are available for all members of staff and visitors.

As well as the energy-efficient skin, other energy-saving features are incorporated into the design, including rainwater-harvesting systems for flushing lavatories and watering the plants, high-performance glazing to control solar energy, and low-energy lighting systems with fittings controlled by daylight sensors. The offices are cooled by a special displacement ventilation system, which uses outside air to cool the building. Biomass boilers supply heating and hot water, with locally sourced wood pellets used as fuel.

In 2011, the Angel Building was short-listed for the RIBA Stirling Prize, Britain's most prestigious architecture award.

30 St Mary Axe, EC3

Standing at a height of 180 metres (591 feet), and colloquially referred to as the 'Gherkin' because of its shape, this elongated elliptical glass tower is among London's tallest structures and is certainly one of its most distinctive. It is a remarkable building in many ways – from the construction of its unique profile to its environmental credentials – and is the product of the Foster and Partners team (see also pages 36, 52, 58, 80, 209). As with many contemporary designs, the building has not been without its critics, but nothing can detract from its sculptural form and its dominance on the city's skyline. It won the RIBA Stirling Prize in 2004.

30 St Mary Axe was commissioned by Swiss Re, a global reinsurance company that needed a building to house their UK head office (although Swiss Re sold the building in 2007). New Building Director Sara Fox was responsible for overseeing the construction of the building, half of which was to be occupied by Swiss Re and the remainder to be leased to other companies. It was built on the site of the former Baltic Exchange, which was erected in 1903 and extensively damaged in 1992, when the IRA detonated a bomb outside the building. Subsequently, the Exchange had to be demolished and space made for this modern statement building, which reflects the City's importance as a financial centre.

Started in 2001 and opened in May 2004, the tower is based on a radial plan, with a circular perimeter that widens as it rises through its 40 floors, before tapering towards the apex. This highly individual design takes account of the limited space of the site; by being narrower at ground level, it provides more room around the base than it would if it were a solid rectangular block; it also creates an optical illusion,

making the structure appear more slender (and therefore less intrusive at ground level) than it actually is. Furthermore, the specific shape of its profile reduces the amount of wind deflected to the ground, so aiming to make it more pleasant for the pedestrian on breezy days. At ground level, retail units open onto a landscaped plaza.

The internal office spaces are arranged around the building's core, with each floor rotated five degrees from the one below. Breaking this dynamic – and a key feature of the internal space – is a series of spiralling light wells that wind around the building and can be seen from outside as dark, tonal bands breaking up the façade of triangular glazing. These wells introduce natural light to the building and

are instrumental in its natural ventilation and insulation processes. The structure is supported by a complicated series of circular steel columns and there is no requirement for internal supports, allowing open-plan floor space. Perhaps surprisingly, the 'glass lens' dome at the apex of the building is the only curved piece of glass in the entire scheme.

The main lobby includes distinctive finishes such as the anodized aluminium wall cladding and stainless steel-covered columns. The top floors (38, 39 and 40), with private restaurant, bar and dining rooms, are privy to some of the most spectacular views over the capital, providing, on the 40th floor, a unique 360-degree view.

Opposite: *The building's distinctive form stands out on the City skyline.*
Above: *The top floor of the building, offering spectacular views over the capital.*

The inspiring concept at the heart of the development plans for Chiswick Business Park was 'Enjoy Work' – the notion being that a happy workforce was a more productive one. In addition, the Park was required to provide an economic and social hub for the local community. Richard Rogers Partnership (now Rogers Stirk Harbour and Partners, see also pages 22, 40, 154, 162), who were commissioned to undertake the design in 1999, took these criteria on board and created a highly positive working environment.

Rather than the usual out-of-town location, this business park lies within a residential area of west London. The 33-acre plot in the suburbs of Chiswick and Acton occupies the site of a derelict bus depot. Due to the immense size of the site and its potential impact on the local community, it was essential that any redevelopment should respond to the needs of both investors and people living in the vicinity. The brief from the developer Stanhope was to create an overall masterplan that could accommodate future changes in the property/business market, while also providing high-quality office space that could be adapted to the needs of different occupiers.

The design, constructed in stages, is based on a series of 12 substantial rectangular buildings arranged in formation around a central, two-tiered lake with a waterfall feature, decked boardwalks and paths, and green spaces. This area provides a particularly pleasant environment for workers or the public to relax in. The scheme involved what was then an unusual approach to business parks by replacing main open-air car-parking areas with landscaping and encouraging employees to use more environmentally friendly means of transport (although some car-parking facilities are provided underneath and behind some of the buildings).

The buildings are very simple in layout. Inside, they consist of a central core around which open-plan offices are situated, and fire escapes are located on the exterior to keep the interior space free. Floor-to-ceiling windows allow plenty of daylight to penetrate into the offices, while

Left: *The buildings in the Park are situated around a lake, with pathways and lawns.*
Opposite: *The reception area, declaring the concept at the heart of the Business Park: 'Enjoy Work'.*

also affording employees views to the landscaped gardens, which create a sense of space and freedom. Aluminium louvres and light-sensitive retractable fabric blinds, both fitted externally, prevent these huge glazed areas from absorbing too much heat and reduce the need for air conditioning.

Although not apparent from the high quality of finish, the construction of the buildings is cost effective, involving a standard precast concrete frame tied to a central steel frame core. The external steelwork is a lightweight tubular structure, with the cladding being mostly glass and the floors concrete. The tubular steelwork creates an intriguing pattern across the surface of the buildings, all of which are very similar in appearance.

To reinforce the 'Enjoy Work' concept behind Chiswick Business Park, there are a number of facilities for employees to use, such as a gym and swimming pool, while the provision of regular social activities, outdoor events and evening classes gives everyone an opportunity to mix and contribute to the community feel.

The Economist Building is part of a complex incorporating three buildings around a raised, small public piazza. It is considered a triumph of 1960s post-war architecture. Located in the traditional environs of St James's Street, it balances modern design with an acknowledgement of the neighbouring 18th-century buildings through its precise and restrained use and detailing of materials such as Portland stone and the regular arrangement of windows. The Economist Building, commissioned by *The Economist* magazine in 1959, is central to the complex and at 15 storeys it is the tallest component of the three. Adjacent is a four-storey irregular polygon mixed-use/office block that fronts St James's Street, and to the rear of the piazza is an eight-storey residential block.

The complex was designed by the husband-and-wife team Peter and Alison

Smithson, who were key and often controversial figures in the avant-garde artistic climate of post-war Britain. They won the commission for this building in a limited competition. The Smithsons had firm ideologies at the core of their architectural designs, and wanted to define a new approach to Modernist architecture that combined the use of cost-effective, mass-produced and prefabricated constructional elements with a simplicity that reflected the influence of Ludwig Mies van der Rohe (1886–1969), German pioneer of Modern architecture. They believed in building structures that were true to their function and location, and were passionate that urban areas should reflect the mixed uses of work, recreation and living space. This was in opposition to the 'zoning' theory popular among leading Modernist architects and the Smithsons' predecessors, such as Le Corbusier (1887–1965) and Walter Gropius (1883–1969), who believed these three areas of human life should be kept separate.

The manipulation of the space between the buildings was also an extremely important factor in the design. The Smithsons situated the three buildings with narrow passageways between them to evoke the character of medieval streets, which still exist in parts of the city, thus adhering to a sense of history while engaging in a contemporary design. The central piazza, which is reached via steps from street level, has a theatrical feel. It provides open public space, but due to its proportions and proximity of the buildings feels secluded and secure.

This appealing complex is often described as reflecting New Brutalism, a phrase the Smithsons regularly used, and one that describes the style and the ideology of the buildings. It is

characterised by rigidly geometric, often repeating forms, and the use of materials such as concrete, often left raw or unpolished. Each of the buildings in the complex is different in size and aspect, but they are all made of concrete, with an emphasis on verticality achieved through upright ribs in between the strongly defined aluminium windows. The corners of the buildings are canted (angled), softening their profile and allowing additional light into the piazza.

The internal office space in the Economist Building was surprisingly traditional in layout and rejected the vogue for open plan. The Smithsons had carried out extensive research with the employees of The Economist and their layout reflected what staff required and desired. At the opening of the building, the editor, Sir Geoffrey Crowther, said that the staff working on the magazine had been nervous on first meeting the Smithsons, but had ended by feeling 'awe and affection' for them.

Opposite: *The use of Portland stone and restrained use of detailing of the Economist Building complements the traditional surrounding buildings of St James's Street.* Above: *The main reception area, showing the architects' distinctive Modernist design approach.*

The Lloyd's building lies at the heart of the City of London — a striking presence on the urban skyline. It was designed in 1978 by the Richard Rogers Partnership (now Rogers Stirk Harbour and Partners, see also pages 18, 40, 154, 162) to house the expanding requirements of the world's largest insurance market, and was completed in 1986. The building is a stimulating example of High-Tech architectural design and was amazingly advanced in appearance for its time, with expanses of glass contrasting with the stainless-steel frame.

This is the eighth Lloyd's home. On the site of the current building stood their 1928 building designed by Sir Edwin Cooper and located on Leadenhall Street. Their next home was by Terence Heysham in 1958 on Lime Street, just across the road. By 1977, Lloyd's had again outgrown its offices and, after talks with a number of architects, the contract was won by Richard Rogers Partnership.

Given the rapid expansion of Lloyd's and the costs incurred through the construction of the previous two buildings, a prime objective for the architects was to create a design with longevity and flexibility in mind, with interior space able to expand and contract to meet the fluctuating demands of business into the 21st century. A further primary prerequisite was to provide a huge, open space for underwriters to conduct their business face-to-face with brokers; this common area, where syndicates agree terms for accepting risk, is known as the underwriting room. The origins for working in a single room like this stem from the 17th century, when Edward Lloyd's coffee house became known as the place for obtaining marine insurance. Finally, the new Lloyd's building had to be an architectural statement reflective of the business and the evolving face of the City.

Cooper's 1928 building was almost entirely demolished to make way for Lloyd's new home, but the original Leadenhall Street entrance was retained and absorbed into the design in a marriage of old and new. The alignment of historic elements into the contemporary design continued with the placement at the heart of the building of the famous 18th-century Lutine Bell, recovered from a wrecked ship. The bell, which hangs in the Rostrum, has traditionally been rung to herald important announcements: once for bad news, twice for good. Today the bell is only rung on ceremonial occasions.

Another, even more, surprising feature is the Robert Adam dining room (1763), which was relocated from Bowood House, the Earl of Shelbourne's home in Wiltshire, to the Lloyd's building in 1958; it was then moved piece by piece to the 11th floor in the current building. The old 1958 building was demolished, and this site is now home to the Willis Building, designed by Foster and Partners (see also pages 16, 36, 52, 58, 80, 209).

Taking account of the irregular site, the Lloyd's Building architects placed all the service areas on the building's perimeter, to retain a clear, unobstructed central working space at the core. This was achieved by designing six separate towers outside the central mass: three to contain lifts (the external ones made of glass), lavatories and pipework, and three as fire escapes — it is these towers that make the structure so distinctive. This was a similar, though more sophisticated, approach to that used in the iconic Centre Georges Pompidou in Paris, designed by Richard Rogers and Renzo Piano and opened in 1977.

The central block is rectangular in shape with concentric galleries looking onto the

atrium, 84 metres (276 feet) high and topped by a vast barrel-vaulted glass roof, which acknowledges the historic precedent of Joseph Paxton's Crystal Palace (1851).

The first four levels are where the underwriting takes place and are open to the central atrium and accessed through criss-crossed escalators, whose fluid, striking design forms an important part of the visual dynamics of the interior. Although spread over different levels, there is a sense of shared, communal space here, heightened through the escalators acting as a central thoroughfare. This level of interaction between workspace and communal space was unusual for the time, but is crucial to both the design and the particular nature of Lloyd's. A distinctive

feature is the rows of artificial lights, which are repeated throughout the building.

All the floors were designed to be adaptable, with the potential to be turned into separate offices or have their internal spaces easily altered.

Visually, the interior space is uplifting. The drama, height and light of the core induces an almost cathedral-like feeling, which contrasts strongly with the dynamic interplay of interior surfaces, shapes and movement and, most importantly, the constant human activity here. Some of the interiors were originally designed by Eva Jiricna, including the Captains' Room restaurant.

Above: *The High-Tech service towers and pipework of Lloyd's are characteristic of the work of the Richard Rogers Partnership.*

Overleaf (left): *Looking down on the central atrium, with its criss-crossing escalators giving access to the first four floors.* (Right) *A dizzying view.*

The Gibbs Building houses the headquarters for the Wellcome Trust – a charitable foundation set up in 1936 to fund research with the aim of improving human and animal health. In addition, the organisation also seeks to promote public engagement on scientific matters and influence health policy across the globe. It was founded on the wealth of American-born Sir Henry Wellcome (1853–1936), who co-founded a highly successful multinational pharmaceutical company, Burroughs Wellcome & Co, in 1880. In his lifetime he funded pioneering medical research, and after his death his will provided for the creation of the Wellcome Trust. He was a true philanthropist as well as an avid collector, and by the time he died he had a huge collection of objects relating to the history of medicine that rivalled those of many famous museums in Europe.

The original Wellcome Trust headquarters were based in a building dating to 1932, but as the Trust expanded they had to occupy various disparate properties in the surrounding area. These offices were mostly cellular, with little opportunity for informal engagement between the organisation's different departments. When the site next door became available, it provided the perfect opportunity to unite the entire Wellcome Trust operation. Architects Michael Hopkins and Partners (see also pages 66, 90) were commissioned to create a design that united two parallel office blocks – one nine storeys high and the other five storeys high and narrower – under a single curved, glazed roof, which encloses a spacious atrium that spans the two buildings and creates an internal 'street'. The work was completed in 2004.

The glass façade is relatively plain, but it forms a significant part of the building's green credentials – it is triple-glazed, with ventilation between the panes, providing great insulating qualities that create a cool layer around the offices in summer, and a warm one in winter. However, the real magic of this building lies in its vibrant interior, with wood finishes contrasting with the steel-and-glass structure. The internal 'street' provides a great sense of community and cohesion while having its own character and identity. It accommodates seating and socialising areas, with *Ficus nitida* trees, as well as a café for staff, an information centre and a number of large meeting rooms. Many of the offices are open to the atrium and open plan. The emphasis on shared space in the building reflects the core values of the Trust – shared scientific endeavour and communication of ideas.

Of particular note is an art installation by Thomas Heatherwick called *Bleigiessen*, which can be found at the western end of the atrium. This enormous piece comprises

Right: The glazed exterior of the Gibbs building with its curved roof.

142,070 glass spheres suspended on wires from the sixth floor. The spheres catch the light and shimmer and glow. This is a highlight of the building and can also be seen by passers-by through the windows.

The original 1930s building, which links directly into the new headquarters, has been refurbished and houses the public functions of the Trust, including an exhibition space, where Henry Wellcome's collection is displayed, a conference centre, lecture facilities and a library. Henry Wellcome would surely have been delighted with the home of the Trust established in his name, as well as the work achieved within it.

Above: *The atrium, with Thomas Heatherwick's art installation,* Bleigiessen, *comprising more than 140,000 glass spheres suspended on wires.*

Former London Underground Head Office, 55 Broadway, SW1

This imposing building, known as 55 Broadway, houses the former London Underground Head Office. In the early 20th century, what was then London Underground was expanding rapidly and a new headquarters was needed to accommodate the increasing numbers of staff on one site. The aim was to create a statement building that would reflect its forward-thinking plans for travel throughout the city and would also be in keeping with their Modernist design philosophy, manifested in its distinctive posters, maps, signs, publications and famous Johnston typeface – all elements of a fully integrated corporate and brand identity. On its completion in 1929, the London Underground Head Office (just above St James's Park tube station) was the tallest building in London, and it is often referred to as the 'first skyscraper'.

The structure was designed by Charles Holden (see also page 172), of architects Adams Holden and Pearson, who designed many Modernist London Underground stations in the 1920s and 1930s. He was awarded the RIBA London Architectural Medal in 1929 for his work on the London Underground Head Office, and in 1936 was awarded a RIBA Gold Medal – a lifetime achievement award to recognise his services to architecture.

The architects had to take account of an awkward site – not only was it irregular in shape, but the District line runs relatively close to the surface, just 7.3 metres (24 feet) below. Holden solved these problems by basing the design on a cruciform (cross-shaped) plan, which made best use of space on the site, and with open-plan offices radiating in four wings from a central tower from the second floor upwards. The upper office floors are stepped back towards a central clock tower at the top, providing a very bold, geometric profile for the building and one that was seen in American office design of the time.

Construction of the offices was based on a steel structure that was supported on a total of 700 reinforced concrete piles. A number of load-bearing steel beams span the railway, and special insulation was used to reduce vibration from the trains. A pale, distinctive Portland stone façade covers the whole of the exterior of the building and, unusually, was left unsanded, so the chisel and cutting marks are still visible. Holden used Norwegian granite for plinth facings and black Belgian marble for the column capitals, along with bronze detailing throughout the interior, giving the building a richly decorated feel.

The outside of the building also features a number of sculptures carved on site by leading contemporary artists, including Eric Gill (see also page 42), Henry Moore and Jacob Epstein (see also page 30).

Two pieces by Epstein – *Night* and *Day* – appear just above street level. They were widely condemned as ugly, primitive and obscene when unveiled. The remaining works appear on the sixth floor, above the pediment, and represent the Four Winds.

Holden created a sense of freedom by making the most of natural light – the cruciform plan provides the optimum level of light into the rooms on the upper floors. Furthermore, he rejected the use of internal solid dividing walls, instead utilising glass panels, which were movable and could be used to create flexible spaces.

Although the building suffered considerable damage during World War II, it was carefully and faithfully reconstructed to restore it to its former glory, under the watchful eye of English Heritage. Today, the ground floor contains a shopping arcade.

Opposite: *55 Broadway was the tallest building in London on its completion in 1929.* Above: *The geometric detailing is in keeping with the Modernist design philosophy of the London Underground.*

Above: *The Modernist exterior of Congress House was intended to embody the progressive spirit of 1950s Britain.* Opposite: *The Conference Hall, with its glazed hexagonal roof lights.*

The immediate post-war years were ones of huge uncertainty and great change – the heart had been ripped out of the country, lives decimated, towns flattened and morale knocked – but, equally, it was a period of great regeneration and hope. In the annual meeting in 1944 of the Trades Union Congress (TUC) – founded in the late 19th century as an umbrella organisation for Britain's trades unions – it was decided to commission a new building to house the institution's headquarters and serve as a memorial to all those members who had died during the course of both World Wars. In addition, the General Council wanted to promote a public interest in the arts and architecture. Congress House, as it was named, was to represent the progressive mindset of post-war Britain – one that was ready not only to embrace change but to effect it. The building was completed in 1957.

The competition for the commission was won in 1948 by David Aberdeen, whose other main work in London was the Swiss Centre in Leicester Square (built 1961–68 and demolished in 2008). His plans for Congress House were, given the conservative nature of the TUC at the time, fairly adventurous, but entirely reflective of the principles of Modern architecture; as testament to the building's success, it is still a piece of landmark Modernism.

Congress House's particular defining element – and that which won Aberdeen the competition – is the ingenious courtyard, which is surrounded on three sides by the office building. Located beneath the courtyard is the Conference Hall (large enough to seat 500), with a roof consisting of glazed hexagonal roof lights set into elaborate leadwork upstands. As a consequence, the courtyard acts as a giant lightwell, allowing natural light into the surrounding offices as well as into the Conference Hall beneath.

The fourth side of the courtyard is taken up by a memorial wall of green mosaic tiles that provide a striking backdrop for an imposing sculpture by Jacob Epstein (see also page 29), who was commissioned to create a war memorial honouring TUC members who had died in both World Wars. Called Pièta, it depicts a woman carrying her dead son and was carved on site from a single 10-ton block of Roman stone.

Continuing the arts theme, there is a large, specially commissioned bronze sculpture designed by Bernard Meadows directly outside the front of the building. In the spirit of the trades union movement, it represents the strong helping the weak.

Congress House is considered among the most important institutional buildings in London and is also one of the most significant of the 1950s. In 1997, Hugh Broughton Architects were commissioned to work with Arup on refurbishing the building, in particular the conference facilities, to allow the building to be used on a commercial basis.

Imagination, WC1

Winner of the UK's Building of the Year Award in 1991, the interior of this building still manages to inspire wonder. The multimedia communications and marketing agency Imagination, founded by Gary Withers, needed a building that would act as the face of the company, reflecting its creativity and strong brand identity. On a practical level, it needed to accommodate a wide range of working spaces, from those for architects, graphic designers, photographers and consultants, to cutting-edge media studios for sound recording, film and video production, and high-end, high-tech events. In 1987, Ron Herron, a leading figure in the avant-garde architectural group Archigram (formed in the 1960s), was commissioned to design the building, working with Imagination.

Rather than start from scratch, Herron came up with an ingenious way of joining two old buildings of differing heights to make one impressive structure. The front building – a tall, red-brick structure, formerly an Edwardian school – appears largely conventional, except for a white fabric 'hat', which can be seen poking up above the roof line. Herron had the idea of connecting this front building to a second one behind it by stretching a tensile fabric roof between the two, including the street that separated them, thus creating a light-filled, five-storey atrium in the middle. Herron was among the first to use this type of fabric roof material, which has since become widespread. Although the idea was Herron's, it was engineering consultants Buro Happold who devised the roof's intricate structure. To maintain its tautness, the fabric was stretched in two directions and divided into a series of peaks and troughs, with an exoskeleton of tension rods and frames supporting them.

Beneath the roof, each floor of the existing buildings is joined through steel and aluminium walkways, the tubular metalwork and latticework adding to the overall visuals of the interior. During the day, this central space has a soft natural light diffused through the fabric roof,

but by night artificial lighting transforms it into a richly glowing, evocative space, often used for functions or events such as fashion shows.

The surprising contrast between this ultra-modern use of space with the outwardly traditional brick building is a juxtaposition that works brilliantly, and provides the perfect home for the innovative company it was built for.

Above: *Looking down on the atrium of the Imagination Building, with its steel and aluminium walkways.*

10 Queen Street Place, EC4

Located at the northern end of Southwark bridge, and overlooking the river Thames and St Paul's Cathedral, this large commercial office building commands some of the best views in London. It is also an excellent example of a structure from a previous era being overhauled to create a contemporary environment to suit 21st-century working practices and principles.

10 Queen Street Place was originally constructed speculatively during the great financial boom of the 1980s, but by the turn of the century it had already become outdated. Seth Stein Architects, John Robertson Architects and HOK (see also pages 84, 85) collaborated on a complete redesign and regeneration of this office building in 2005, and the following year the project was given the London Regional British Council for Offices (BCO) Award for Refurbished/Recycled Workspace.

The re-envisaged building was taken over by leading international law firm S. J. Berwin, who moved here in 2006, and it is the core principles of this organisation that underlie the fundamentals of the new design. The need to create a working environment that embraced transparency was paramount, alongside a sense of community among staff.

At four storeys high, this building might not appear vast at street level, but each of these storeys encompasses one acre of floor space. In addition, the fourth floor has been extended and a huge, landscaped roof terrace added. This roof terrace is a particularly successful part of the redesign, affording spectacular views, as well as providing a serene piece of open space far above the busy London streets. It is used for formal or informal socialising and events, or simply as an area for relaxation, helping the building strike the right balance between accommodating the high pressures of a busy working environment with the essential need for escaping those pressures, if only for a short period. As such, 'breakout areas', or spaces for meetings, socialising and relaxing, have also been created alongside the office space.

A striking feature of the redesign is the double-height entrance lobby, which, with its clean and ultra-modern interior immediately sets the character of the building. This space is dominated by a light installation, the colours of which can be altered for certain occasions or events, bringing visual variety to the building both during the day and at night. Other noteworthy additions have been the new main lift and, most impressive, the series of atria throughout that allow natural light to penetrate right to the heart of the structure and make pleasant informal meeting spaces. Two of the three atria also contain elegant spiral staircases. All the private offices and the larger meeting rooms on the first floor are fronted by either clear or translucent glass, to encourage an environment of transparency and openness.

Above: *Clear and translucent glass helps to create a feeling of transparency and openness.*

120 Fleet Street, former Daily Express building EC4

The façade of the former *Daily Express* building, with its black glass and vitrolite, chrome frames and curved corners, makes this one of the capital's most distinctive structures. It is also one of the best surviving examples of Art Deco architecture in the city, and the original curtain-walled exterior was the first of its kind in London.

Newspaper baron Lord Beaverbrook commissioned Sir Owen Williams to design a building to house the huge *Daily Express* newspaper enterprise in 1930 (completed in 1932). As Beaverbrook guessed, the black-glass sheathing would prove particularly effective at night, the lights indicating that his journalists were at work on the next day's paper. The chief specification was to have a single uninterrupted basement space to accommodate the printing presses for what was, at the time, the biggest-selling newspaper in the world, and all other design aspects radiated from this. Taking account of this, Williams (who was an engineer by training) designed a pioneering concrete structure that allowed for an expansive, open-plan floor space.

The superb entrance hall, designed by English architect Robert Atkinson, was inspired by American Art Deco cinemas; certainly, it evokes a sense of Hollywood luxury. The floor featured a wave pattern made of blue and black rubber rimmed with green, while the ceiling above was ornamented with gold and silver leaf. The walls, which were covered with travertine tiles and finished with a rosewood dado, featured two large decorative plaster reliefs by Eric Aumonier depicting Britain and its Empire. Silver and gilt predominated, including a large, silvered pendant lamp.

The newspaper industry declined during the 1980s and the building closed in 1989, standing empty for seven years before undergoing redevelopment. Despite a considerable rebuild, the façade and entrance hall were saved and have been restored by specialists Plowden Smith. They have reinstated some features, including the wave-patterned floor and the spectacular silver leaf details on the ceiling. Aumonier's panels have been restored, and hidden uplighting installed that illuminates these and the ceiling. Fixtures such as silver serpent handrails have also been reinstated. Today, this is one of the most exuberant entrance halls in London.

Above: *Black glass sheathing distinguishes the building's exterior, while* (right) *the interior is one of London's best surviving Art Deco examples.*

City Gate House & 50 Finsbury Square, EC2

The Bloomberg UK Headquarters is a prominent presence on Finsbury Square, at the edge of the City of London. In 1991, the international media corporation Bloomberg moved into the 1920s City Gate House, designed by Sir Giles Gilbert Scott (see also page 78) as a gentleman's club. In 1997, the building was transformed internally by Powell-Tuck Associates, and in 2000 Bloomberg expanded into the adjacent building (50 Finsbury Square), designed by Foster and Partners (see also pages 16, 52, 58, 80, 209). The traditional aspect of the square imposed a number of design limitations on the architects, who nonetheless succeeded in capturing the progressive spirit of the corporation.

Among the planning constraints imposed on the design was a requirement for the office block to be made of stone, which would be in keeping with the surrounding buildings. The architects' solution was to create a slender, elegant stone frame enclosing a largely transparent glass cube that houses the offices inside. The stone exoskeleton has a classical rhythm to its structure, which adheres to the need for a traditional aspect, but does so with striking modernity.

The Finsbury Square façade is of particular interest, with a distinctive entrance defined by a diagonal stone wall that juts from the building's right-hand corner to the doorway. This single piece of solid, uninterrupted concrete is a diversion from symmetry and lends weightiness and substance, seeming to pin the building to this pivotal corner. The top two floors of the same façade are set back, with a terrace in front; not only does this set-back terrace act as a key design feature, but it was a neat way of satisfying the building-height regulations. Similarly, the roof curves away from the adjacent building to avoid blocking its natural light.

The interiors were designed by Powell-Tuck Associates, with the aim of encouraging interaction between staff and stimulating creativity. High ceilings and vast expanses of glass create an environment lacking in visible barriers, and a series of glass bridges acting as walkways help to create an airy, energising feel. The unique combination of television studio with office space is visible immediately on entering the atrium, giving direct views into the studio and displaying Bloomberg's multimedia and marketing services onto a glazed wall. All the offices are open plan and each floor has its own colour, represented in the fittings. Tropical fishtanks, art installations and floral displays are also key elements of the design.

In May 2002, the company opened Bloomberg SPACE, a gallery dedicated to commissioning and exhibiting contemporary art, within the Bloomberg office building but open to the public.

Above: *A stone frame encloses the glass cube of the building.*
Opposite: *High ceilings, expanses of glass and internal bridges create a working environment that promotes transparency, creativity and interaction.*

BT Tower, W1

London's skyline is defined by several immediately identifiable buildings, of which the BT Tower (formerly known as the Post Office Tower) is one. With its main structure 177 metres (581 feet) high, this was the tallest building in the United Kingdom from the time of its completion in 1965 until 1980. Despite its obvious imprint on the skyline, the tower was classified as an official secret until 1993, and up to that time had not appeared on any Ordnance Survey maps.

The BT Tower was the first purpose-built structure to transmit high-frequency radio waves and was commissioned by the General Post Office (GPO) in 1961 to facilitate telecommunications from London to the rest of the country. It was opened in October by the then Prime Minister, Harold Wilson. It is still in use as a major communications hub, and also carries broadcasting traffic between

television broadcasters and international satellite services.

The narrow, cylindrical tower was designed by the chief architect of the Ministry of Public Works, Eric Bedford, and architect G. R. Yeats, and rests on a concrete raft that forms the foundations some 8 metres (26 feet) below the ground. A hollow concrete shaft runs from ground level through the centre of the tower, acting as a stabilising backbone; it is further anchored through attachment to an adjacent four-storey building. Typical of its time, the tower was constructed in concrete faced with specially tinted glass to prevent overheating. It is able to withstand slight expansion

and contraction due to changing weather conditions of up to about 23 centimetres (9 inches), and will move no more than 25 centimetres (9¾ inches) in abnormally high winds. Two high-speed lifts transport visitors to the top part of the tower, taking just over 30 seconds to reach the 34th floor.

In addition to the telecommunications space and offices, the BT Tower provided public viewing galleries, a shop and a rotating restaurant when it was opened. The restaurant, housed on the 34th floor, took 22 minutes to make a full revolution and was a popular tourist destination. However, in 1971 a bomb, claimed by the IRA, was detonated in the men's lavatories in the Top of the Tower Restaurant. Sadly, for security reasons the restaurant was closed for business in 1980, the year its lease expired, and public access to the building was stopped in 1981.

While the tower is visually striking, the architecture also manages to reflect the building's stark functionality. The BT Tower is best appreciated at night, due to the impressive LED lighting display that wraps around the 36th and 37th floors at a height of 167 metres (548 feet). The display, which is currently the largest in the world of its kind, acts as an information band, and from October 2009 provided a countdown to the 2012 London Olympics.

Opposite:
An unmistakable silhouette on London's skyline.
Above: *The remarkable view from the 34th floor of the tower.*

In 1990, the Richard Rogers Partnership (now Rogers Stirk Harbour and Partners, see also pages 18, 22, 154, 162) were commissioned to design the new home for the broadcasting company Channel 4, and the building was opened in 1994.

The form of the building was prompted by the site, on the corner of Horseferry Road, in central London. It consists of two four-storey wings, arranged in an L-shape and joined by a curved connecting block that comprises the foyer. This central block, which is the most dynamic part of the building, has a four-storey, frameless, concave glass façade and is flanked by two satellite towers, which are clad in pewter-grey aluminium. The tower to the left contains four conference rooms, one above the other, while the right-hand tower houses lifts and utility areas. The reddish-brown steelwork on the outside of the building contrasts with the aluminium cladding and glass.

From the street a ramp of steps leads over a glass bridge to the building's entrance. The bridge crosses over what initially appears to be a pool, but is in fact a roof light that defines the circular foyer of the cinema below.

Inside the building, the tall, narrow foyer, with its vast expanses of glass, creates an airy, uplifting atmosphere. Plate glass and glass blocks were used throughout the building, to reduce its impact in a built-up area and to afford views to the outside world. At the back of the foyer, half a level down and running along its curved length, is a restaurant overlooking a landscaped garden. This eating area forms the heart of the social and community elements of the building, and is open only to Channel 4 staff. A rooftop terrace extends from the boardroom to overlook the garden.

The two wings contain mostly offices, accommodating around 600 staff. These separate wings are linked through tiers of elegant walkways, crossing over the foyer space at each floor level. Emphasis has been placed on texture and materials throughout the building, and the walkways are no exception. These were constructed from concrete with punched-out areas of glass, which form an interesting pattern, particularly when seen from above and below. The external cladding also has bands of light mesh acting as sun screens.

Outside, the impressive entranceway is marked by a 15-metre (50-foot) high metal sculpture of the number four, leaving little doubt to the building's occupant. This huge sculpture mirrors the television channel's on-air logo and was constructed in 2007 as part of their 25th anniversary, and to launch the 'Big Art Project'. Since then, many artists have provided 'skins' for the piece to reflect their own artistic ideals and is something that the passing public can enjoy.

The building, with its contemporary design, glass structure and Hi-Tech detailing, entirely reflects the spirit of Channel 4 – a relatively young television station that is associated with creativity, experimentation and innovation.

Above: *A stepped ramp and glass bridge lead to the concave glass front of the building.*
Opposite: *Elegant walkways cross over the foyer space at each level.*

Above: Old and new complement each other in form and materials.
Opposite: View of the atrium with spiral staircase, during Phase 2 of construction.

Broadcasting House, headquarters of the BBC and one of the first purpose-built broadcasting centres in the world, is a highly recognisable and somewhat contentious building that is both dearly loved and criticised by the public. The original building, designed by British architect (George) Val Myer in 1932, was a bold Art Deco statement; over the last 10 years or so, major restoration work has been carried out and two grand extensions added, with a new public piazza at the centre of the development. Broadcasting House has a strong, powerful presence, which is further heightened by its position directly opposite the elegant Regency All Souls Church, designed by John Nash.

The original Art Deco building is faced in white Portland stone. At its heart is a studio tower flanked with offices to provide noise insulation, and floor-to-ceiling windows line the façade at ground level along the Portland Street side; the original intention was to rent out the ground floor to retail units and restaurants to help fund the construction costs, but the BBC expanded so rapidly it ended up using the space itself. For its time, the original building was highly advanced, not only for its recording and transmission functions, but also in its use of air conditioning and artificial daylight in rooms without windows. The interiors were designed by Raymond McGrath. A notable feature of the exterior is the statue of Prospero and Ariel (both characters from Shakespeare's play *The Tempest*) over the front entrance, made by Eric Gill (see also page 29).

In 2002, the BBC decided to extend Broadcasting House. The aim was to increase efficiency and reduce long-term costs by bringing national and international journalism, national radio and music services together under one roof. Following a major architectural competition, MacCormac Jamieson Prichard (now MJP Architects) were selected to carry out the work.

The redevelopment project was a two-phase programme, with the initial phase being a restoration of the original building and the construction of a new extension to the east, called the Egton Wing, which was opened in 2006 and contains studios and offices. Like the original building, the new façade was clad in Portland stone.

The second phase, which was started in 2005 and completed in 2011, consisted

TEMPLVM·HOC·ARTIVM·ET·MVSARVM·ANNO·DOMINI·MCMXXXI
RECTORE·IOHANNI·REITH·PRIMI·DEDICANT·GVBERNATORES
PRECANTES·VT·MESSEM·BONAM·BONA·PROFERAT·SEMENTIS
VT·IMMVNDA·OMNIA·ET·INIMICA·PACI·EXPELLANTVR
VT·QVAECVNQVE·PVLCHRA·SVNT·ET·SINCERA·QVAECVNQVE
BONAE·FAMAE·AD·HAEC·AVREM·INCLINANS·POPVLVS
VIRTVTIS·ET·SAPIENTIAE·SEMITAM·INSISTAT

Above: The 1930s entrance hall with its distinctive Art Deco design.

of a large, glass-fronted wing, which is linked to the other two buildings and houses the Newsroom. MJP devised the initial design, but this was adapted by architects Sheppard Robson, who were required to scale down the ambitious plans and saw the building through to its completion.

Visitors to the building enter via the large, open-air piazza, where they walk over a map of the world, engraved with place names and criss-crossed with lines of longitude and latitude. Created by artist Mark Pimlott, this is one of many newly commissioned art works at Broadcasting House, and acts as a reminder of the BBC's global presence as provider of news to 285 million people worldwide.

The new entrance, sited at mezzanine level, has views directly into the massive Newsroom – which is the largest of its kind in the world. Framed by four colossal pillars, this cavernous space features spiralling staircases, which are made of oak, glass and steel, and huge lift shafts painted in bright, bold shades of red and orange.

In 2013, over 5,000 members of staff will move into Broadcasting House from their offices and studios elsewhere. Accessibility is key to the design, and from 2013 the public will be able to see the journalists at work from a viewing gallery, to experience something of the buzz and excitement of life in a newsroom. The outdoor piazza will double as a performance and exhibition space, and a café and bar will provide a unique opportunity for the BBC staff and audiences to mingle.

Abbey Mills Pumping Station, E15

Abbey Mills Pumping Station A, the first sewage pumping station to be built on the site, was designed 1865–68 by engineers Joseph Bazalgette and Edmund Cooper, and architect Charles Driver (see also page 46). Described as 'the Cathedral of Sewage', this hugely important building managed to achieve an elegance and beauty that is not necessarily associated with sewage stations. The latest addition to the Abbey Mills sewage complex, Station F, designed in 1997 by Allies and Morrison, balances simple, understated design with modern aesthetics.

A rectangular, industrial, barn-like building, Station F raises the level of incoming sewage by 12 metres (39 feet) and pumps it along its route east towards the processing plant at Beckton. Construction was centred around a steel base, with lightweight A-frames forming the upper structural parts and giving rise to the distinctive shape of the roof. The A-frame construction is visible externally on the gable ends and forms part of the strong geometry of the exterior. Inside the station, a square steel frame supports the travelling cranes used for maintaining the pumping chambers, which are located deep below ground level.

The outside of the structure is clad in zinc-coated aluminium panels; louvres along the ridge of the roof, with a dull silver iridescence, provide ventilation to the building. These belie the nature of its function and render its appearance temple-like, in keeping with the splendour of Pumping Station A.

Left: *The strongly geometric exterior form of Station F with its zinc-coated aluminium cladding, and* (above) *the elegant yet functional interior.*

Crossness Engines House was designed as a direct result of the Great Stink of London in 1858. The combination of an exceptionally warm summer and a horrendously polluted river Thames, into which the city's untreated sewage flowed, created a stench so vile that sacks soaked in deodorising chemicals were placed at the windows of the House of Commons; cholera and typhoid outbreaks were frequent and deadly. Victorian legislators were forced into action, and the engineer Joseph Bazalgette (see also page 45) of the London Metropolitan Board of Works (MBW) was finally able to put his plans for a new sewage system into action.

Central to the plans was the construction of intercepting sewers to the north (Northern Outfall Sewer) and south (Southern Outfall Sewer) of the Thames and adjacent to the river. To service these sewers, Bazalgette and architect Charles Driver designed the Abbey Mills Pumping Station (see page 45) on the Northern Outfall and the Crossness Pumping Station on the Southern Outfall.

The Crossness building is largely Romanesque in style, constructed in gault (a mixture of heavy clay and sand) brick, which gives it a pale creamy yellow colour, enlivened by red-brick detailing such as arches and string courses (narrow projecting horizontal bands). The overall impression is of a monumental building that is not obviously industrial. The main entrance doorway, now hidden by an extension, was defined by a red-brick archway and decorated with the MBW coat of arms and those of surrounding counties, while three side-entrance doorways are defined by similar arches. Originally, the Crossness building was dominated by a towering chimney, which has since been demolished.

While the exterior is of note, it is the interior that astonishes, largely due to its vast proportions, which lend it a similarly cathedral-like character as Abbey Mills Pumping Station A. It is also richly ornate, with intricate wrought and cast ironwork throughout, most of which is painted in bright colours. The centre of the space is taken up by an elaborate octagonal structure of tall iron columns, supporting iron screens set in arches and panels that incorporate the MBW monogram; the elaborate decorative scheme of the ironwork represents foliage, leaves and fruit. Located in the corners of the building are the four engines built by James Watt and Co. – the largest surviving engines of their type in the world.

In the 1950s, the pumping station was decommissioned and allowed to fall into a serious state of disrepair, also suffering at the hands of vandals. However, the building was granted a reprieve in 1970, when it was awarded a Grade I listing to reflect its historic importance, and in 1987 the Crossness Engines Trust charity was established to manage restoration work. Funding by a number of organisations, including Heritage Lottery Fund, English Heritage and the Homes and Communities Agency, has allowed the Trust to embark on a programme of work that includes much-needed restoration to the main buildings, a new access road to the site and improved facilities for visitors, including an exhibition area.

Opposite: *A surprisingly ornate and brightly coloured interior of wrought and cast ironwork* (above) *is barely hinted at by the Romanesque façade* (below).

A small pocket of land in the east Docklands, on the northern bank of the Thames and opposite the Millennium Dome (now the O2 Arena), is home to a vibrant melding of history and innovation: Trinity Buoy Wharf Container City, sited in a district once so important to Britain's shipping industry, has recently been the subject of an unusual regeneration programme.

Trinity Buoy Wharf was established in 1803 as the Thames-side workshop for Trinity House, to produce life buoys and develop lighthouses, lighthouse training and lightships. During the Victorian era, numerous buildings were constructed on the site, including the surviving Electrician's Building (1836) and the only remaining lighthouse in London, Bow Creek lighthouse, built by James Douglass in 1864–66. It was here that scientist Michael Faraday (1791–1867) carried out many of his experiments. The Wharf remained active until 1988, in which year it was closed and sold to the London Docklands Development Corporation. In 1996, however, the site was taken on by Urban Space Management to regenerate the area into a centre for the creative arts, with exhibition spaces, workshops, studios, room for the performing arts, cafés and living space.

One of the most exciting aspects of this redevelopment is Container City, a project that has seen old shipping containers recycled into bright and affordable live/work spaces. The aim was to create new studio space at a construction cost low enough to ensure affordable rents. It was built in two phases – City I in 2001 and City II in 2002, of which the most recent development, the Riverside Building, was finished in 2005.

City I is four storeys high, and all the containers are painted a red-brown colour.

Above: Re-used shipping containers form the structure of Container City – a bright collection of work/live spaces for creative professionals (below).

City II, which is five storeys high and painted in vibrant primary colours, was built adjacent to the first block; the two are linked through connecting bridges and a vertical area formed by two 'towers' (containers turned on their end), which contain a lift in one and stairs in the other. Round windows in each of the containers create an almost nautical look, reminiscent of portholes – appropriate for the dockside location. Sliding glass doors replace the containers' double metal doors at the end of the units, although the original metal doors remain in place but are secured open and support a balcony above. In City II, some of the units also have side balconies,

providing outdoor space.

To ensure the containers were habitable, the inside walls and ceilings were sprayed with insulation (over a waterproofing membrane) and then covered with plasterboard; meanwhile, interior space was enlarged by joining two or more containers through removal of internal walls and insertion of steel supports.

Container City has proved a cost-effective and innovative answer to the difficulties of providing housing and workspace in modern society. It offers a light, clean, ecologically sound and stimulating environment.

The UK Supreme Court
Gray's Inn
Royal Courts of Justice
HM Treasury
Home Office HQ
Lancaster House
Royal Danish Embassy
Marlborough House
Portcullis House
Custom House
Bank of England
Foreign Office & India Office
Guildhall
Barking Town Hall
City Hall
Walthamstow Town Hall
BMA House
RSA
Royal College of Physicians
Haberdashers' Hall

GOVERNANCE AND POWER

'London has always been about renewal. What reflects this spirit better than its architecture? You may not like all of it but the best shines through, from whatever age.'
Open House London visitor

As the capital of the United Kingdom, London has for centuries housed the major political and legal state institutions, which remain among the most recognisable features of its urban landscape. Historically, their architecture is symbolic, reflecting the power and authority invested within: large, imposing and often richly decorated buildings with great presence, in prominent locations. The Guildhall and Custom House in the City of London, the Royal Courts of Justice, and the major governmental buildings clustered in and around Whitehall are among the best examples of this tradition. This is continued to a lesser degree in the headquarters of the many professional associations, societies and guilds in the capital.

The commitment to preserve the nation's most significant historic buildings can sometimes conflict with the need for a fully functioning, modern working environment. However, many government buildings, including the Foreign and Commonwealth Office, HM Treasury and the medieval Guildhall, have undergone careful restoration and adaptation by leading contemporary architects, to convert them into workspaces for the 21st century while recognising their continuing role as physical embodiments of the British State. Not all buildings currently in use by government or legal institutions were originally built for this purpose, but have instead been drafted into service because of their suitability. These include the grand Lancaster House, which was originally built as a private home in the early 19th century, but is now used for entertaining visiting foreign officials and dignitaries, and the UK Supreme Court, which was the old Middlesex Guildhall until it was extensively remodelled in 2003 to make the building suitable for its new judicial role.

London's complex regional political system is also evident in many other fine surviving examples of local and regional government buildings. The creation of municipal boroughs in the 19th and early 20th centuries led to the building of new civic halls throughout the capital, including Barking Town Hall and Walthamstow Town Hall, which were both commissioned in the 1930s. The influence of early Modernism on these designs aligns with the new civic status of these boroughs, and their aim of being seen as progressive and enlightened governing authorities.

London's more recent government buildings reflect changing attitudes to power. City Hall, on the south bank of the Thames, was the result of the need for a new building to house the recently appointed Mayor of London and the London Assembly (together comprising the Greater London Authority), established after a referendum in 2000 and now accountable for the strategic government of Greater London. The design brief for this vast glass structure, opened in 2002, was to create a building for the GLA that would become a new landmark for the capital, with an internal helical ramp giving views into the offices and debating chamber, symbolising the transparency of the democratic process.

In 2003, the British government announced plans to form a Supreme Court – the final court of appeal in the United Kingdom for civil and criminal cases, and where cases of the greatest public and constitutional importance are heard. This meant a suitable building needed to be found – one that was large and impressive, befitting the highest legal authority, as well as easily accessible to the public. The former Middlesex Guildhall fitted the bill; forming a quadrangle with the Houses of Parliament, the Treasury and Westminster Abbey, it could not have been in a more prominent location and was also sufficiently spacious and grand. Archaeology has revealed that the building stands on the site of a 13th-century belfry, part of Westminster Abbey, where fugitives could seek refuge from their accusers.

The first Middlesex Guildhall building was constructed in 1889 to house the Middlesex County Council. However, the Council soon outgrew its space so commissioned Scottish architect James Gibson to create the present building between 1906 and 1913. The brief was for a building that would both complement its neighbours and have a distinct character of its own; to meet these requirements, Gibson presented an eclectic design that is principally Victorian Gothic in style, but with Art Nouveau elements.

The exterior's most distinctive features are its corner turrets, parapets and dormer windows, which resemble those on the Houses of Parliament, and the abundance of ornamental statues, carved by English sculptor Henry Fehr, on the façade. Rising above the prominent entrance portal is a tower with large, arched windows. In keeping with the medieval theme, Gibson used a considerable amount of stained glass throughout, including in the two large

internal courtyards he designed to bring light into the building.

In the 1980s, the Guildhall was converted into a Crown Court, and seven criminal courtrooms were created from the existing space. During this conversion, many of the original features of the building were covered up; most significantly, the amount of natural light coming into the building from the courtyards was compromised, making the interior dark.

Between 2007 and 2009, conservation architects Feilden and Mawson, supported by Foster and Partners (see also pages 16, 36, 58, 80, 209), embarked on an extensive programme of restoration to make the building suitable for a Supreme Court. The focus was on enhancing the historic fabric of the building, and sensitively reversing many of the more recent adaptations that left it feeling gloomy and cluttered. The imposing, adversarial atmosphere of the Crown Court also had to be converted into an environment suited to Supreme Court business: learned discussion of points of law rather than trial by jury.

The two main rooms on the ground floor, both previously courtrooms, were carefully restored, and today they house

Above: Court 2 is the most modern of the three courts.
Opposite (above): The entrance hall's glass panels feature the Supreme Court's emblem and quotes from the Judicial Oath.
(Below): The prominent entrance portal features ornamental statues carved by Henry Fehr.

the Supreme Court Library, with its fan-vaulted ceiling, and Court Three, with its stained-glass windows. Likewise, the original Council Chamber on the second floor was converted into Court One and its decorative, carved ceiling has been carefully conserved. The courtyards were cleared of many years of equipment and debris, making the interior considerably lighter, and many features were restored, including the wooden panelling, carvings, stained glass and pieces of historic furniture, which were moved into the reclaimed courtrooms. A new courtroom was also added.

As well as undertaking restoration work, the architects reorganised space to make the building more user-friendly and to open up public access – for example, the brick vaults, once serving as prison cells, have been transformed into a contemporary-style café and exhibition space. For those interested in law, it is worth noting that members of the public are welcome to observe court cases – an opportunity to gain a fascinating insight into the workings of the British legal system.

The buildings, courtyards and gardens of Gray's Inn have a history stretching back over 700 years, although the general style and layout of the buildings reflect significant Georgian influence, following extensive rebuilding in the 18th century. They invoke a sense of quiet grandeur, reflection and study entirely in keeping with the site's historic function.

The Honourable Society of Gray's Inn is one of the four Inns of Court responsible for the education of student and post-call barristers in England and Wales. All student barristers must belong to one of the four Inns (the others being Lincoln's Inn, the Inner Temple and Middle Temple) that 'call' students to the 'Bar' as barristers once they have successfully completed the Bar Professional Training Course. Today, Gray's Inn incorporates extensive offices for barristers, accommodation, a chapel and historic hall as well as many administrative buildings. It is organised into two principal squares, with the remainder situated along the perimeter of the gardens.

The origin of the Inn of Court dates back to the late 13th or early 14th century. Records indicate that the first building on the present site was the Manor of Purpoole, belonging to Sir Reginald de Grey (died 1308), Chief Justice of Chester and Constable and Sheriff of Nottingham, and the de Grey family is thought to have leased the Manor to a society of lawyers some time around 1370. Certainly, by the prosperous era of Queen Elizabeth I (1558–1603), Gray's Inn was a large, thriving Inn of Court that was closely aligned with the statesmen of the day, and owing to its prosperity subsequently became associated with culture, refinement and entertainment as well as law – William Shakespeare is said to have performed here at least once.

Three serious fires during the 17th and 18th centuries destroyed many of the buildings, including the library, so extensive rebuilding followed; by 1774, one of the only original buildings remaining was the Hall – the true heart of Gray's Inn. During the 15th and 16th centuries, the students undertook their training and ate meals here. Today, the Hall is still used for Calls to the Bar, dining, and social and theatrical events.

Despite serious bomb damage in 1941, which affected much of Gray's Inn, some of the Hall's interiors survived, including the 16th-century stained-glass windows and art works that had been moved to

Left: *Due to extensive rebuilding in the 18th century, the style of Gray's Inn has a significant Georgian influence.*

Left: *The library was among the buildings that were rebuilt after being destroyed by fire during the 17th and 18th centuries.*

safety. The rebuild was undertaken in the late 1950s by architect Sir Edward Maufe, who recreated the timber-framed, Gothic roof and raised dais of the Hall, then reinstalled the original long table, windows and panelled walls that had been in storage. At the west end of the Hall is a large wooden screen, said to have been given to the Inn by Elizabeth I and carved from the wood of a Spanish galleon captured during the Spanish Armada. Maufe also rebuilt the chapel, reinstating the original stained-glass windows, including one featuring Saint Thomas à Beckett; this had been

removed in 1539 to appease Henry VIII, who ordered the destruction of Beckett's shrine at Canterbury Cathedral during the Dissolution of the Monasteries.

Part of the charm of Gray's Inn is the garden, which stretches over five acres and is one of the largest private gardens in London. Called the Walks, it was designed in 1606 by Sir Francis Bacon, who was Treasurer of the Society. The gardens have changed through the centuries, but the elegance of the manicured space offers a small corner of peace in the centre of London to this day.

Monumental in scale, the Royal Courts of Justice – which house the Court of Appeal and High Court of Justice for England and Wales – is one of the finest examples of Victorian architecture in London. It is located in a prominent position on the Strand, where it rises to three storeys, although the abundance of towers, spires and pinnacles of different heights create an irregular and distinctive roofline.

The idea to build new premises for the Royal Courts of Justice (then known simply as the Law Courts) was proposed in 1866, and the same year Parliament opened a competition for architects to submit plans. The commission was eventually awarded to architect and former lawyer G. E. Street. Unfortunately, Street died before his grandiose design for the courts was finished, allegedly from the stress of the project, but his son, Arthur Street, and the architect Arthur Blomfield completed his scheme.

G. E. Street's principal architectural interests lay in the Gothic style, and he was considered an expert in this field, having written a number of books on the subject and produced many detailed drawings of medieval buildings he had visited in England and on the Continent. Unsurprisingly perhaps, his love of 13th-century architecture is very much in evidence in his design for the Royal Courts, for example the rib-vaulted ceiling and tall, stepped lancet windows. Construction began in 1873 and took eight years to complete, with Queen Victoria officially opening the building in December 1882.

The building's function is immediately represented in the figures around the elaborately carved porch, which features past judges and lawyers and a dog and a cat, symbolising litigants in court.

Alongside these secular figures are Jesus, Moses and Solomon – reminders of humility, divine law and wisdom respectively, and the existence of justice at a higher level.

To either side of the main entrance are smaller gateways that lead to several courts, as well as waiting rooms for the jury and witnesses, with separate staircases that take them directly to their boxes in court. The courts are much as they were when they were first built, and each one has a different decorative scheme. There are also robing rooms, where members of the Bar don their wigs and gowns, and consultation rooms, where lawyers can advise their clients.

The most impressive feature of the interior is undoubtedly the Great Hall, one of London's most magnificent Victorian interiors. Built in the manner of a cathedral nave, the hall is a vast 25 metres (82 feet) high and almost 73 metres (238 feet) long, embellished by soaring arches and an exquisite mosaic-tiled floor. The windows are stained glass and feature the coats of arms of various Lord Chancellors and Keepers of the Seal, whose portraits line the walls. In total, there are over a thousand rooms in the building, reached by almost 6 kilometres (3½ miles) of corridors, many of which still have their original oak panelling and carved wooden detailing.

Only 30 years after the completion of the Royal Courts more space was needed, and plans for the first extension – the West Green building – were drawn up. Since then, there have been a number of other extensions as well as structural changes and some refurbishment to the interior. Despite this, the original character of the Royal Courts of Justice remains firmly intact.

Opposite: *The Great Hall, built in the style of a cathedral nave, stands a vast 25 metres (82 feet) high.*

Following the Norman Conquest in the 11th century, the Treasury (responsible for managing royal finances) was moved from Winchester to London's Whitehall, which now contains all the major government buildings. As one of the major departments of state, the Treasury has remained there ever since, although it has been in its current building only since 1940.

This huge edifice was originally built to house other government departments and was designed principally by the Scottish architect John Brydon in two phases between 1898 and 1917. Alongside what is now HM Treasury, the building also houses parts of the Cabinet Office, and its reinforced basement is home to the Cabinet War Rooms, Winston Churchill's wartime bunker from where he directed World War II with his cabinet.

The basic design for this government office building is relatively simple and fairly symmetrical, consisting of two halves linked by a courtyard. Each half of the building has its own smaller courtyards, or lightwells. The west end, on Parliament Street, was completed in 1908, and the east end, on St James's Street, in 1917. The distinctive, circular central courtyard was based on a design by English architect Inigo Jones (1573–1652) for a new Whitehall Palace, which was never built. Jones was one of the most influential architects of his day – he was the first to bring Italianate Renaissance architecture to England, and his legacy includes several prominent buildings in London, including the Banqueting House in Whitehall. Sadly, many of his buildings were destroyed in the Great Fire of London in 1666.

Although this is a magnificent historic building, the original layout of the interior did not make best use of available space,

which became a problem as the Treasury expanded and more offices were required. As a consequence, Foster and Partners (see also pages 16, 36, 52, 80, 209) were commissioned in 1996 to redevelop the interior, to make the most of available space and create an updated workplace suitable for the 21st century.

One of the key aspects of the redesign was to cover the smaller courtyards with glass roofs. In so doing, the architects created a number of five-storey-high indoor spaces that serve a variety of functions, including a new entrance atrium, a library, training rooms and a café. Other internal courtyards and the main central courtyard were landscaped, with the introduction of pools and plants to create pockets of recreation space within the building. Furthermore, over 11 kilometres (7 miles) of internal partition walls were removed from the offices to optimise space and create large, open-plan working areas. By 2002, when the refurbishment was complete, all the members of the Treasury could be housed in the western half of the building, freeing up the eastern half for other departments.

HM Treasury is an excellent example of an historic building that has been given a new lease of life through sensitive and imaginative redevelopment, making it a more efficient, open and flexible place to work.

Opposite: *The entrance atrium, with a clear view of each storey of the building.*

The Home Office building at 2 Marsham Street is located on the former site of the demolished Departments of Environment and Transport, known as Marsham Towers (and colloquially as 'the toast rack' or 'the three ugly sisters'). The new structure was built as a Private Finance Initiative deal with construction company Bouygues UK and Ecovert, with the cost to be spread over 29 years.

Building began in 2002, and took just over 34 months to complete. Driven in part by a government strategy to reduce the number of buildings in the Home Office estate, the focus for the architects, Terry Farrell, was on providing a flexible and organic workspace. To this end, the open-plan offices are naturally lit and easily accessible, based off three central atria and looking out onto turfed outdoor 'parks' where staff can sit during breaks. Each floor also has two breakout areas, providing ample space to engage in informal meetings. The exterior of 2 Marsham Street has a coloured-glass façade running along its length, designed by Liam Gillick, which, depending on the weather, tempers the incoming natural light.

The site comprises three buildings, each named after prominent figures in the Home Office's history — Seacole, Peel and Fry — and staff circulate between the three via a bridge known as 'The Street', which forms a corridor linking the three locations from the first to fourth floors.

The consultancy firm Advanced Workplace Associates studied how Home Office employees used their workstations to establish the most effective use of space in the building. As a consequence much of the existing furniture was retained and a system was introduced whereby staff now move between desks, rather than having one set space to work at. With this more effective use of space, 4,500 staff now occupy the site, compared to 3,800 prior to the redevelopment.

2 Marsham Street is designed as a vibrant space determined by the nature of the people and the business within it, and is a thoroughly contemporary demonstration of flexible working space.

Above: *The vibrancy of the coloured glass façade of 2 Marsham Street continues inside the building* (right), *with naturally lit offices and flexible workspace.*

Above: *The grand central hall of Lancaster House, with its marble-lined staircase.*

Lancaster House, now managed by the Foreign and Commonwealth Office (see pages 72–75) and part of the St James's Palace complex, was one of the last great stately homes in London in the neo-classical style. Built in mellow, honey-coloured Bath stone, the house was commissioned in 1825 by the Duke of York – second son of George III and heir to the throne – and designed principally by English architect Benjamin Dean Wyatt.

The Duke of York died in 1827, before the house had been finished. However, the building was bought by the extremely wealthy George Leveson-Gower – later the 1st Duke of Sutherland – who saw the house through to its completion. He retained the services of Wyatt, but rather unusually also employed a number of other architects, including Sir Robert Smirke (see also page 69) and Sir Charles Barry (see also pages 205, 206), best known for his involvement in the redesign of the Houses of Parliament.

The internal layout of the house is arranged around a grand central hall and staircase (lined with marble and with a very heavy cast-iron balustrade), and contains three floors of principal rooms plus a basement with service rooms and staff quarters. The most impressive rooms in the house are the State Rooms on the first floor, which were used primarily for entertaining; the less formal family rooms were on the ground floor and family bedrooms on the second floor. The interior decorative scheme – in the opulent Louis XIV style, with gold leaf and rich textures – reflected their lavish tastes and set a precedent for stately London residences for many years to come.

The Sutherland family were known for their liberal politics, love of the arts and prodigious entertaining, and many distinguished guests stayed at the house.

In 1913, the Lancastrian soap-maker Sir William Lever (later Lord Leverhulme) bought the house and renamed it Lancaster House – a reminder of his northern roots; the same year, he gifted it to the nation. For many years, the house was home to the London Museum, and since the end of World War II it has been used primarily as a centre for government receptions and as a filming location for a number of music videos and films, including *The Young Victoria* and BBC's *Churchill at War*.

Royal Danish Embassy, SW1

The Royal Danish Embassy is a bold statement of modernist Scandinavian design, yet it looks remarkably at home slotted among the more historic buildings (mainly 19th-century mansion blocks) along Sloane Street.

The commission to design the Embassy was awarded to Danish architect Arne Jacobsen, who is remembered as one of the first Scandinavian architects and designers to introduce Functionalism to Denmark. This aspect of his style is keenly felt in the London embassy, reflecting the purpose for which it was designed while remaining sympathetic to the surrounding buildings. Jacobsen died in 1971, six years before the Embassy (the only building he designed in London) was completed, and the design was taken over by the Danish architectural firm Dissing and Weitling, with the structural aspects of the build taken on by engineers Arup.

Recalling the fact that the site was previously occupied by a terrace of houses, the building has been divided vertically into five large bays, which retain the pattern of the old walls and provide a feeling of symmetry along the entire street frontage. The ground floor is recessed, and above this rise three storeys of bold black aluminium 'boxes' with rounded corners; the top two storeys, which are also set back, house the ambassador's residence. To the rear of the embassy is a row of mews-like buildings, created from a single row of pods arranged with a classical regularity, which provide housing for staff.

The metal cladding and detailing of the exterior is currently painted grey-green, which is not how Jacobsen envisaged it. Originally, he wanted the exterior to be a pale, sandy colour to fit in with some of the adjacent buildings faced in sandstone (his chosen pale colouring can still be seen in parts of the interior). He had also specified bronze panels on the exterior, but at the time of construction these were considered too expensive.

Opposite: *The pattern and rhythm of the Embassy's Functionalist façade is bold yet responds to the surrounding architecture. The interior (left) has a restrained yet welcoming feel.*

The Royal Danish Embassy is a particularly good example of 'defensive architecture', with the issue of security being evident in the design of the exterior. Most notably, the ground floor has no windows; instead, separating the building from the traffic at ground level is a wall made of distinctive, rough concrete panels depicting an abstract design by 20th-century Danish painter and sculptor Ole Schwalbe. In front of the wall is a row of simple but solid, rectangular stone planters. The entrance also has echoes of a defensive nature: single storey and two bays wide, above it hovers a huge solid panel almost two bays in width, which suggests a modern variation on the historic drawbridge. Once inside, however, the building has a welcoming feel. From the main entrance, a glass-enclosed metal staircase leads to the offices on either side of central corridors on the second, third and fourth floors – the fifth and sixth floors contain the residence, directly accessible from the courtyard. In 2001, the former exhibition/lecture hall was converted into the Embassy of Iceland, with a separate entrance.

Through his design, Jacobsen managed to perfectly fulfil all of the criteria required for an embassy while creating a modern architectural classic in the heart of Belgravia.

The large, red-brick building located to the east of St James's Palace on Pall Mall is one of the less ornate royal mansions, but it fulfilled the request made by Sarah Churchill, Duchess of Marlborough (1660–1744), for a building that was 'strong, plain and convenient'. This prestigious site was one of two given to John Churchill, 1st Duke of Marlborough (1650–1722), by the Crown in recognition of his victories on the Continent as leader of the Grand Alliance forces in the War of the Spanish Succession (1701–14), the other being an estate in Oxfordshire where he built the grand Blenheim Palace. His wife, Sarah, who was for a time a great confidante of Queen Anne, did not want to live in such an ostentatious building and set about influencing the designs for Marlborough House to reflect her more modest tastes.

Sarah commissioned Sir Christopher Wren and his son (also called Christopher) to design Marlborough House. A strong-willed woman, she was a driving force in the planning of the building, and laid the foundation stone on 24 May 1709; later, after a disagreement with the Wrens, she oversaw the completion of the mansion (in 1711) herself.

Originally, Marlborough House was two storeys high, but two further floors were added in the mid-19th century. The red Dutch-brick façade with white stone detailing is highly distinctive – the bricks had been used as ballast in the ships that transported the Duke's soldiers from Holland back to England after the third Anglo-Dutch war (1672–74). The interior has been altered over the years. However, at the heart of the interior is Wren's original double-height, nearly square salon that is lined with paintings by the French decorative artist Louis Laguerre, depicting the Duke's battles including the Battle of Blenheim. The ceiling has a cupola surrounded by exquisite paintings by Italian baroque artist Orazio Gentileschi, which originally hung in the Queen's

Left: *A dignified exterior, fulfilling the Duchess of Marlborough's requirements.*
Opposite: *Sir Christopher Wren's salon, lined with paintings by Louis Laguerre.*

House, Greenwich. The battle theme continues in paintings that hang along the paired staircases leading from either side of the Salon to the first floor.

The Dukes of Marlborough occupied the house until 1817, when it became a royal residence. Between 1849 and 1863, the building was used for various public functions, including housing the Vernon and Turner picture collection, part of the National Collections. In 1863, alterations were made to the building by English architect James Pennethorne, including the new north wing and the enlargement of a number of the principal rooms to prepare it for occupancy by the Prince of Wales,

later Edward VII, who lived there between 1863 and 1901.

In 1959, Queen Elizabeth II offered Marlborough House to the British government as a Commonwealth Centre. Today, the building is home to the Commonwealth Secretariat and the Commonwealth Foundation, an organisation that services the 54 Commonwealth countries – all independent states working together in the interests of its citizens. Conferences and summit meetings of Commonwealth Heads of Government take place here, and it has been the venue for several independence negotiations.

Portcullis House, SW1

In the late 1980s, the architects Michael Hopkins and Partners (see also pages 26, 90) were commissioned to carry out a space audit of the whole of the Parliamentary estate, which revealed a serious shortage of office space and committee rooms. It was decided that a new government building was necessary to accommodate over 200 Members of Parliament and their staff. Named after the portcullis used to symbolise the Houses of Parliament on official documents and stationery, Portcullis House was designed 1992–93 and opened in 2001.

The site, on the corner of Victoria Embankment and Bridge Street, was also the location of London Underground's proposed Jubilee Line extension and a new interchange at Westminster tube station. Consequently, the two projects (Portcullis House and the new Underground station) were devised simultaneously by the same architects; Portcullis House sits above the seven-storey-high underground chamber of the station, with six columns providing primary structural support to both the station below ground and much of the building above.

This RIBA-Award-winning building represents a clever solution to the problem of slotting a contemporary building between two historic public landmarks – New Scotland Yard (1890) and the Houses of Parliament (completed in the 1850s). The design of Portcullis House clearly echoes features found in its neighbours – principally a strong emphasis on verticality and the steeply pitched roof and chimney design – while offering its own interpretation of a contemporary government building. The chimneys are not only aesthetically appropriate but they also provide a sophisticated, energy-efficient ventilation system.

Above: The distinctive 'chimneys' provide an energy-efficient ventilation system.
Opposite: The arching oak and glass roof and landscaping define the central courtyard.

The floor plan for the new government building is based on a rectangular layout of five principal storeys and two attic floors positioned around a central courtyard. At ground level, the two street frontages have an open arcade extending along their length, incorporating a row of retail units and the Underground station entrance. A secure underpass links Portcullis House to the Houses of Parliament, so MPs can go from their offices to the House of Commons to vote when Parliament is in session without going outside.

The building is perhaps best appreciated from the inside. Its defining element is the central courtyard, with its remarkable two-storey-high, arching oak and glass roof and indoor landscaping. Housing two restaurants, a coffee shop and an e-library (an enquiry point where MPs and staff can use networked computers to access information), the courtyard is used mainly by MPs and their staff and forms the social hub of the building. The upper floors contain committee rooms – where Select Committees meet to scrutinise the work of the government – and offices for MPs, with each floor unofficially allocated for different political affiliations.

Portcullis House has been built to withstand terrorist attacks, and its fortified appearance and construction materials – including the reinforced, bomb-proof external cladding – reflect this.

For hundreds of years, maritime trade and shipping were crucial to Britain's economic success, with the Custom House – the building where government officials processed paperwork for the import and export of goods – playing a fundamental role in the industry's administration in London.

There has been a tradition of custom houses on this site on the north bank of the Thames since 1275, when the first building was established to collect dues for King Edward I. Replacements were constructed in 1378 and 1559. Thereafter, the site experienced a run of misfortune through the centuries, particularly in the number of fires that destroyed the buildings. The first was the Great Fire of London (1666), which burnt Custom House to the ground. Sir Christopher Wren (see also page 64) was commissioned to design a new building, which was completed in 1671, overlapping with his planning of St Paul's Cathedral. However, Wren's building was severely damaged in a gunpowder explosion in 1714, so Yorkshire-born architect and Surveyor for the Office of Works, Thomas Ripley, was commissioned to design yet another new building, which was completed in 1775. Only 39 years later, fire broke out once more, resulting in the construction of the Custom House that survives today.

The current building was designed 1812–17 by David Laing, Architect and Surveyor to the Custom Board. The primary objective was to create more space to house the greatly expanding customs office brought about by massive growth in Britain's sea trade. Continuing the run of bad luck, the central portion of Laing's building collapsed in 1825,

Opposite: *Custom House is sited on the north bank of the Thames.*
Left: *The simple yet elegant interiors are still used for their original purpose.*

and he was subsequently sacked from his post. Architect Sir Robert Smirke (see also page 61), who produced a report on the inadequacy of Laing's original build, was awarded the job of rebuilding the damaged portion, carried out 1825–27.

The façade, which consists of a large central portico flanked by two smaller projecting sections, is relatively unadorned, except for the 12 Ionic columns, with their scroll-like ornamentation. These references to classical architecture, combined with the monumental scale of the building, serve to create an impression of power by association – typical of buildings housing official institutions – and continues through to the interior.

Smirke created a new entrance hall, with stone stairs at either end that lead to the Long Room on the first floor. One of the

most important rooms in the building, and based on earlier designs by Ripley and Laing, the Long Room faces the river and occupies the entire length of the central portion of the building. In its day, this large gallery contained the public offices of the Customs Service and it was where all paperwork regarding duties payable on cargoes was presented to customs officials. Most notable in Smirke's Long Room are the simple, unadorned Tuscan pilasters and the gently curved ceiling, over 16 metres (54 feet) high. The ground floor and basement were originally used for storing impounded goods. The offices in the east wing were badly bombed in World War II, but have since been recreated in replica.

The long history of Custom House continues today, as the building is still in use by HM Revenue and Customs.

The imposing, neo-classical, Grade I-listed building that houses the Bank of England occupies a huge site of three-and-a-half acres in the heart of the City of London. Affectionately referred to as 'the Old Lady of Threadneedle Street' – a name derived from a satirical political cartoon published in 1797 – this vast building now rises seven storeys above ground level and has a further three basement levels, which contain the cavernous bullion vaults.

The Bank of England was founded in 1694, and its role is fundamental to the United Kingdom's economy, committed as it is to promoting and maintaining the nation's monetary and financial stability. It acts as banker to both the British government and other banks, manages the country's foreign exchange and gold reserves and has the monopoly on issuing bank notes; since 1995, it has also been responsible for setting interest rates in the United Kingdom.

The first purpose-built home for the bank was designed by George Sampson, Surveyor to the Bank, and constructed on the Threadneedle Street site between 1732 and 1734. This building was greatly expanded by sculptor-turned-architect Sir Robert Taylor (see also page 96) in 1765–88, who built a central rotunda in the main banking halls, to allow light through.

Taylor's use of top-lighting was greatly advanced by Sir John Soane – Architect and Surveyor to the Bank and one of the greatest architects of his day – who made considerable improvements on the building between 1788 and 1833. These included the new banking halls, or salons, each of which was lit from above through side-lit domes resting on arches, and the addition of internal courtyards to allow further light in. The interiors of

Soane's banking halls were decorated in a classical style, and his work on the Bank of England greatly influenced the design of commercial buildings thereafter. Another feature added by Soane was the defensive curtain wall around the building.

In an act that architectural historian Sir Nikolaus Pevsner described as 'the worst individual loss suffered by London's architecture in the 20th century', nearly all of Soane's additions to the building were demolished and a new building designed by Herbert Baker was constructed between 1925 and 1939. Baker retained the outside wall and followed Soane's general layout in his redesign of the banking halls, but he vastly increased the dimensions of the building, turning it from three storeys to seven and adding the three basement levels, which between them have more floor space than the nearby Tower 42 (formerly

the Nat West Tower), one of London's tallest buildings.

Baker's grandiose façade has a vast portico of columns sculpted by Charles Wheeler. This includes a number of female figures (called the Lothbury Ladies), the gilded finial figure of Ariel – who represents the dynamic spirit of the Bank carrying credit and trust throughout the world – and the 6-metre (20-foot) high bronze doors.

The majestic scale of the architecture, both outside and inside, leaves no doubt as to the magnitude of this building and reflects the Bank of England's pivotal role in managing the nation's wealth. A museum on the premises, which is open to the public, tells the fascinating story of the Bank from its foundation to the present day. There is also a private garden within the grounds – a small oasis in the heart of the City.

Opposite: *Herbert Baker's grandiose façade with its vast portico of columns.*
Above: *The richly decorated interiors reflect the significance of the Bank of England as one of the nation's key institutions.*

The stately white Italianate building between Parliament Street and St James's Park in Westminster once housed four separate government departments – the Foreign Office, India Office, Home Office and Colonial Office (latterly known as the Commonwealth Office). Today, it is occupied solely by the Foreign and Commonwealth Office (FCO) – a government department headed by the Foreign Secretary that promotes the interests of the United Kingdom overseas. It is an unmistakable statement of power that extends from the façade through to the restored interiors.

The building dates to 1858, when Sir George Gilbert Scott (see also page 208) was awarded the commission to design new premises for these major government departments. Initially, Scott proposed plans in the Victorian Gothic style, but these were rejected by Prime Minister Lord Palmerston, who insisted on a classical style as he strongly disliked Gothic architecture. Construction started in 1861 and finished in 1875.

Arranged around a large quadrangle containing four smaller courtyards, the layout consisted primarily of three main storeys, plus a basement and attic level. The Home and Colonial Offices were based in the eastern wing, near Whitehall, the Foreign Office in the north west and the India Office in the south west, looking onto the lake in St James's Park. The four departments each had their own, distinct identity, which was reflected in the architecture: the Foreign Office and India Office were highly ornate, designed to impress foreign visitors and be a statement of British power, while the Colonial Office and Home Office were viewed as functional working spaces, with less ostentatious interiors.

Scott's design for the interior of the Foreign Office was opulent, particularly the grand State Stair, with its wide, carpeted steps and marble balustrade that leads to the first floor. The ceiling is richly decorated with gold and the opulence continues into the Grand Reception Rooms (also known as the Locarno Suite): the Cabinet Room, Dining Room and Conference Room, the last with a heavily gilded ceiling and painted ceramic plaques featuring the arms of 20 different countries.

The Grand Reception Rooms were built primarily for the purpose of entertaining foreign dignitaries, but acute shortage of space meant they were used as offices during World War I. In 1925, the Treaties of Locarno were signed here, with the principal treaty – between Germany, France and Belgium, with the United Kingdom and Italy acting as guarantors – concerning the preservation of the countries' borders to avoid war. During World War II, the same rooms were used by the Cyphering Department for code-breaking, and after the War, they were divided up with plasterboard partitions and turned into further much-needed office space.

The India Office was set up in 1858 to oversee the administration of colonial India – represented in the statues of eminent Indian statesmen situated in niches along the façade. The interiors, designed by Sir Matthew Digby Wyatt, Surveyor of the former East India Company and later Architect to the Council of India, were especially elaborate, most notably the Council Chamber, with its palatial proportions and heavily gilded decorative scheme, which aptly reflected the room's importance. Highly decorated, carved furniture, doors and the large marble chimneypiece were moved over from the former home of the Office in East India

Opposite: *Sir George Gilbert Scott's State Stair, with wide, carpeted steps and marble balustrade.*

House, Leadenhall Street. Although the chairs and tables have now been transferred to the India Office Library at St Pancras in order to preserve them, some original mahogany chairs, a newspaper stand and the Chairman's seat remain *in situ*.

One of the finest aspects of the India Office is Durbar Court – an impressive courtyard at the heart of the building, with a marble floor and surrounded on all four sides by three storeys of arches and red and grey granite columns. The courtyard was originally open to the sky, but an iron-and-glass roof was erected in the 1860s to make it suitable in all weathers. Durbar Court was first used in 1867, for a reception for the Sultan of Turkey; the adjoining Council Chamber was transformed into a dining room and draped with sheets of silk and regimental standards and, reputedly, every piece of tableware was made of gold. The courtyard was also a venue for some of King Edward VII's coronation celebrations in 1902. After 1947 – the year of India's independence from Britain – the India Office ceased to exist as a separate ministry, and it was taken over by the Foreign Office.

In 1963, with the Foreign Office battling space issues due to expansion, it was suggested that the original Scott building should be demolished to make way for new offices. The resultant public debate, however, led to the building being awarded a Grade I listing, and an extensive programme of refurbishment was implemented. The Home Office moved out in 1978 and the building was unified internally, with the four previously separate parts being brought together as a single building to house the Foreign and Commonwealth Office. Between 1984 and 1997, a restoration and refurbishment programme was carried out that provided

25 per cent extra usable space for far less than the cost of demolition and rebuilding, and the key rooms were restored to their original splendour.

Overleaf: *Durbar Court, the impressive courtyard at the heart of the building.*

Guildhall, EC2

Since the Middle Ages, Guildhall has been the administrative centre of the City of London government. The Anglo-Saxon word *gild* translates as payment, so it is also possible that the building was originally where citizens came to pay their taxes.

Built by master mason John Croxton between 1411 and 1440, this architectural masterpiece is the only secular stone structure in the City to have survived the Great Fire of London in 1666. However, it was not the first guildhall building – documents dating to 1128 refer to a guildhall in London, and it is likely the present building was constructed on the same site or close by. There are remains of a 13th-century gatehouse at the entrance, and the crypts that lie below the main hall (the largest medieval crypts in London) are certainly older than the principal

structure, with the East Crypt dating to the 11th century and the West Crypt to the late 13th century. Archaeological excavations undertaken in 1987 revealed the remains of a huge Roman amphitheatre, considered the largest in Britain; today, part of the outline of the arena is marked by a slate circle set into tiles in the courtyard in front of the building.

Croxton's design produced the Great Hall, which forms the heart of the building and – at 46 metres (152 feet) long, 15 metres (50 feet) wide and 27 metres (89

feet) high – is a truly vast space. Through its history, the Hall has been used for state trials, notably in 1553, when Lady Jane Grey was convicted for high treason, and in 1606, when the English Jesuit Henry Garnet was tried for his association with the Gunpowder Plot. Both were found guilty and later executed.

At each end of the Hall, huge Gothic windows take up most of the wall space, and the side walls feature Romanesque windows that record previous Lord Mayors of London, starting with the first, Henry

Fitz Ailwyn, in 1189. The interior features a number of monuments to national heroes, including the Duke of Wellington, Admiral Lord Nelson and Sir Winston Churchill. It also contains carved wooden figures of two legendary giants, Gog and Magog – the traditional guardians of the City of London. During the annual Lord Mayor's Show, huge wicker versions of these two giants are traditionally carried in a ceremonial procession.

The arched, stone roof – the fifth roof on the Main Hall – was designed in 1953

Opposite: *The Porch in the Guildhall Courtyard.*
Above: *The 11th-century East Crypt predates the principal structure.*

its grandiose turrets the porch is loosely Gothic in style, but is also somewhat reminiscent of Indian architecture.

Another architect who has been strongly connected with the Guildhall is Sir Horace Jones. Architect and Surveyor for the Corporation of the City of London between 1864 and 1887, Jones was responsible for several prominent buildings, including Billingsgate and Smithfield Markets, Guildhall School of Music (which has since become Guildhall School of Music and Drama and moved to a new building in the Barbican) and Tower Bridge. As well as building the fourth roof for Guildhall's Main Hall (which was destroyed in the Blitz), he designed the Old Library building, which housed the Guildhall Library and Museum, and the impressive Livery Hall.

Originally, the Old Library (the second one at Guildhall) was lined with oak bookcases and housed over 40,000 books and maps, but in 1974 the collections were moved to a newly constructed west wing (designed by Robert Gilbert Scott, the son of Giles). Built in 1969–75, Scott's west wing accommodates the current L-shaped library and new offices, and now forms the main entrance to the Hall. Today, the Old Library is used as a reception room, and although the collections are no longer there, visitors can still enjoy the room's proportions and striking stained-glass window depicting 15th-century writer, diplomat and printer William Caxton.

Guildhall continues to play an important role in the City. Housing the offices of the City of London Corporation, it is a fully operational town hall, where the Court of Common Council – the City's primary decision-making assembly – meets monthly. Many of the rooms are used regularly for state and civic banquets and ceremonies, as well as for corporate and private entertaining; and the Art Gallery, added in 1999, accommodates the City of London's highly regarded collection of art. It is a truly civic building in every sense.

Above: *Sir Horace Jones designed the Old Library building, which housed the Guildhall Library and Museum.*

by architect Sir Giles Gilbert Scott (see also page 36), grandson of Sir George Gilbert Scott (see pages 72, 208) and best known for his work on Battersea Power Station, Liverpool Cathedral and the power station that is now Tate Modern. The exterior of the hall has also been altered since Croxton's day – the most obvious addition being the deep, four-storey porch on the south façade, added by the prominent English architect and surveyor George Dance the Younger, in 1789. With

Barking Town Hall, IG11

In the 1920s, the population of Barking grew rapidly – many people were escaping the slum conditions in London's East End, and new public housing developments were built to accommodate the newcomers. In 1931, the Ford Plant at nearby Dagenham was set up, bringing further development to the area. The same year, Barking (which had been an Urban District) became a Municipal Borough, and it was evident a town hall was needed – something more prestigious and progressive in style to replace the former Victorian building in East Street.

The commission was awarded to architects Herbert Jackson and Reginald Edmunds in October 1936. Their plans were ambitious and necessitated the demolition of a series of buildings between Barking Broadway and Axe Street to accommodate the new Town Hall. Construction began immediately, but by the time World War II broke out, only the basement area had been completed. Building work was stopped, but the basement was utilised as an air-raid shelter and to house the headquarters of the Air Raid Prevention Group.

Construction did not begin again until 1954. The first part of the building to be completed was the main block, whose exterior has changed little. This comprised the municipal offices and civic suites, and was made from distinctive small red bricks, with window surrounds and the entrance portal picked out in white stone. Most of the windows are simple, Georgian sash-style, while others are more elaborate with balconies. The clock tower rises up above the central portion of the main block and has an Art Deco-style clock face on each side, with the shaft of the tower punctured with a vertical row of tiny windows that recall ancient defensive openings.

Between 2000 and 2004, a few years before plans were unveiled to regenerate the Barking Town Centre, architects Hawkins Brown refurbished the Town Hall to upgrade it for present-day use. They added a number of features that have greatly enhanced the building – most notably, a barrel-vaulted, illuminated glass bridge that spans the entrance hall, which adds drama to the space and introduces daylight. This is further complemented by a specially commissioned, striking blue-and-white, Art Deco-style mural, 3 metres (10 feet) high and 5 metres (15 feet) across, created by London-born artist J. P. Trevor. Entitled *Berecingum and Deccanhaam* (the old Saxon names for Barking and Dagenham), the mural depicts key historical events, landmarks and architectural features from this area of east London.

Left: *The entrance hall, featuring an Art Deco-style mural by J.P. Trevor.*

Situated on the south bank of the river Thames, the unmistakable new City Hall, designed by Foster and Partners (see also pages 16, 36, 52, 58, 209) and opened in 2002, is one of London's most recent landmark buildings, with its unique, rounded outline, clearly delineated floors and glass structure.

City Hall is part of the 'More London' development, which aimed to regenerate a site that had remained undeveloped for decades with a mix of uses including offices, a hotel, a health club, shops, bars, restaurants, a children's theatre and open public spaces. The building was designed to house the new Mayor of London and the London Assembly – with its 25 elected members who scrutinise the work of the Mayor and represent the interests of Londoners – as the Greater London Authority, the wider strategic regional body.

The democratic aspect of City Hall's activities was fundamental in the design process, and the resulting building – with its extensive use of glass both inside and out – places enormous emphasis on transparency and accessibility, bringing the public into close proximity with the workings of the democratic process in order for them to feel involved.

Unusually for an important government building, there is no discernible front or back to City Hall, and the entrance on the riverside leads into a ground-floor foyer area with a distinctive chrome ceiling. Reflecting the exterior, the interior is based on a spiral form centred on a gently sloping, stepped spiral ramp that ascends up and around the middle of the building, with all the offices and rooms located radially from the ramp. At the heart of the building is the Assembly Chamber, through which the ramp also spirals.

On the top floor is what is sometimes referred to as 'London's Living Room', where an open viewing deck around the building affords spectacular views across the capital. On the lower-ground level is a public café that looks out onto a large, open space in the form of an outdoor sunken amphitheatre. Known as the Scoop, the amphitheatre is open to the public and during the summer months often stages events such as open-air concerts.

A large part of the building's optimum energy performance is based on the spherical shape, which has 25 per cent less surface area than a cuboidal building of the same volume. As such, there is a minimal surface area exposed to sunlight. An innovative cladding and glazing system that allows for shading and natural ventilation also helps. On the south side, the building leans back, resulting in the floors being stepped inwards so each storey affords shading to the one beneath.

Below: City Hall's unusual rounded form sits on the south bank of the Thames.

Opposite: The spiral ramp ascending up the building was intended to bring visitors into close proximity with the work of the Greater London Authority.

The striking Town Hall complex in Walthamstow was designed in 1932 by P. D. Hepworth, who won a competition for the commission (and a further prize of £500, which was a substantial amount at the time). The competition was generated when Walthamstow became a London borough in 1929 and required a prominent civic hall to reflect its changed status. Construction began on the building in 1937, but by the time World War II broke out it was still only a shell; it was eventually completed in 1942.

The complex comprises the Town Hall at the centre, with the Walthamstow Assembly Hall to the east and the Magistrates' Court to the west. These buildings are arranged within a formal landscaped setting with flower beds and a fountain that adds to their presence, while behind is a grassed area called Chestnut Fields.

The most dramatic of the three structures is the Town Hall, which is monumental in dimensions, its bulk emphasised through the simple, solid design. The horizontality of its layout is balanced vertically through the central portico – with its four unadorned columns that extend to the full three storeys of the building – and the tall, square, green clock tower that rises from the flat roof. As was common in civic buildings in Britain in the 1920s and 1930s, the design of the façade is based on an austere style of Scandinavian modern architecture known as Nordic Classicism. Hidden beneath the foundation stone at the main entrance is an airtight chamber containing keepsakes from the late 1930s and documents that detail the hopes and aspirations of Walthamstow's citizens at that time – secrets that have yet to be uncovered.

With the War putting pressure on the nation's finances, the interior was

completed more simply than Hepworth had originally intended – plywood panelling was used in the committee rooms instead of oak, and terrazzo floor tiles in place of marble in the foyer. There was also a planned sculptural frieze by artist Francis Cavanagh, a pupil of Henry Moore, for the entrance, which was never executed. However, Cavanagh did carve five figures that were intended as a tribute to designer and craftsman William Morris (1834–96), member of the Pre-Raphaelite brotherhood, who was born in Walthamstow. Despite limited funds, the interior is still visually interesting, particularly the historic Council Chamber, which was once a courtroom and is now used for functions.

The Assembly Hall, which was also designed by Hepworth, was finished in 1943. Renowned for its excellent acoustics, the hall has attracted international stars such as Sir Yehudi Menuhin, Jessye Norman and Placido Domingo.

Opposite: *The monumental façade of the Town Hall belies a more simple, though no less interesting interior, including the historic Council Chamber* (above).

For over 85 years, BMA House has been the national headquarters for the British Medical Association (BMA), the professional organisation for doctors in the United Kingdom. In addition, it provides office space for around 200 other businesses and organisations. The building was originally commissioned by the Theosophical Society – an American spiritual and philosophical organisation founded in 1875. English architect Sir Edwin Lutyens' wife, Emily, was a follower of the Theosophists and introduced her husband to the Society's President, Mrs Annie Besant, who subsequently asked him to design a suitable headquarters.

The foundation stone was laid on 3 September 1911, but the relationship between Lutyens and Besant was turbulent, mostly due to the Society not having the funds to finish the house according to the architect's vision. By the outbreak of World War I, only part of the building was complete and it was taken over by the Ministry of Munitions of War. By the end of the War, the Theosophists had run out of money and the incomplete building was bought by the BMA in 1923. Lutyens was recommissioned to finish the project, and it was officially opened in 1925. Since then, over 40 different architects have worked on the building to extend and modernise it, from the addition of a main entrance building by Cyril Wontner Smith in 1927 to the recent refurbishment by HOK (see also page 34) in 2008.

The original part of the building is neo-classical Palladian in style, described by Lutyens as 'Wrenaissance', after the great London architect Sir Christopher Wren (1632–1723). The façade is distinctive, made from red brick and pale Portland Stone, with a green Westmorland slate roof. The chief Lutyens' rooms are the Great Hall, which had originally been conceived as a temple for the Theosophists, and the John Snow Room and Sir James Paget Room.

The Great Hall is, as one would expect, the centrepiece of Lutyens' design, although at one point in its history it was used as a badminton court for staff, and it has since

been subdivided to accommodate a library with committee rooms occupying the roof vault. The hall was intended to have a vaulted ceiling, but it was never completed because of the expense. However, the room is still large and ornately decorated, with its red-and-gold-painted columns and beamed compartmented ceiling.

The central courtyard houses two memorials. The first is the impressive cast-iron Gates of Remembrance, designed by Lutyens to honour the 574 BMA members who died in World War I. The second, which was designed in 1954 by sculptor James Woodfood, consists of a central fountain surrounded by commemorative statues, which together form a memorial dedicated to the medical men and women who lost their lives in World War II. Lutyens also designed a garden, filled with medicinal plants. The site has literary connections – a commemorative plaque indicates the foundations of the 18-roomed Tavistock House, the family home of novelist Charles Dickens between 1851 and 1860.

HOK's 2008 refurbishment was undertaken at the request of the BMA to turn the 'fine rooms' of the building into a conference venue. The architects preserved and restored the best of the traditional designs, while undertaking a programme of modernisation, which involved creating a new entrance and reception, a 300-seat conference auditorium, a business centre, meeting rooms and a much-needed circulation route on the ground floor. This renovation returned the building to the showpiece it once was, while adapting it to meet 21st-century needs.

Opposite: *The central courtyard, with the cast-iron Gates of Remembrance.*
Above: *The Great Hall, which forms the centrepiece of Edwin Lutyens' design, sympathetically updated for the 21st century by HOK.*

Founded in 1754 by artist, inventor and social reformer William Shipley, the Royal Society for the Encouragement of Arts, Manufactures and Commerce (RSA) is an organisation committed to tackling social challenges faced by man in the 21st century. The Fellowship consists of 27,000 members from a wide variety of disciplines, who undertake research and development projects, meet up to propose and debate innovative ideas and solutions, and work with partners to implement positive change.

In 1774, the RSA moved into the building where it remains today. It was specially designed for the organisation by Scottish architect Robert Adam as part of the Adelphi Buildings scheme (a block of neo-classical terrace houses, most of which have since been demolished). At ground level, a relatively unassuming portico marks the entrance. However, from the

first floor up the façade becomes a great deal more imposing, with a very large, Venetian-style window dominating the centre, flanked by four Ionic columns, two on either side and each two-storeys high, supporting a pediment with a stone figure.

The entrance hall, renovated in 1922 by eminent architect and architectural historian Arthur Bolton, includes art works by the 19th-century English painters Charles Cope and John Callcott Horsley (who invented the Christmas card). The main rooms are on the first floor, most notably the Great Room, which is reached through its own entrance chamber. It is dominated by a series of six vast paintings entitled *The Progress of Human Knowledge and Culture*, painted especially for the room by Irish artist James Barry in 1777–87. Above the room, which now acts as a lecture theatre, is a glass-domed roof.

Also on the same floor are several other, smaller rooms, which are used for meetings and functions. These include the small, intimate Drawing Room and the larger Romney Room, which retains the original Adam ceiling. The Adelphi Room – once a fashionable dining room, as mentioned in Charles Dickens' novel *Pickwick Papers* – is still very much in character of the Adam style. The building was one of the first in London to be fitted with electric light, which was installed in 1882 and incorporated current obtained from a dynamo driven by a gas engine.

Below the building are the Vaults, originally built as riverfront warehouses and wine cellars, and leading directly to the Thames. These brick vaults, which form four interconnecting spaces, were developed in 1990 by Sam Lloyd, of Green Lloyd Architects, to serve as the Fellows' restaurant. The Vaults are connected to the rest of the building through the atrium, also built by Lloyd. Above the Vaults is the

Opposite *The neo-classical façade is notable for its Venetian-style window.*
Left: *The atrium, designed by Sam Lloyd, connects the Vaults to the rest of the building.*

lower basement, which was originally a tunnel-like thoroughfare that connected the Strand to the river Thames. This area was converted into a small theatre in 1990 and retains its brick facing and original flagstones under the seating.

A refurbishment project in 2011–12, directed by Matthew Lloyd (see also page 141), aims to convert some of the ground-floor areas into more flexible space to provide for a greater range of events, and to further improve the Great Room.

Established in 1518, the Royal College of Physicians (RCP) supports and represents its members and monitors the medical profession to ensure the highest standards of medical care; it also advises the government on public health matters. The College has been housed in several buildings throughout its long history – including its previous headquarters in Trafalgar Square, in what is now Canada House. In 1958, Sir Denys Lasdun, the eminent English architect probably best known for his work on London's National Theatre, was commissioned to design a new building to house the expanding organisation.

The present headquarters is located next to Regent's Park, on the site where a war-damaged house designed by John Nash (1752–1835) had been demolished. Nash was an Anglo-Welsh architect responsible for much of the layout of Regency London, including Regent's Park and its surrounding grand neo-classical terraces, crescents and villas. Lasdun's aim was to deliver a bold statement of Modernism while producing a building that was sufficiently impressive to represent the historic institution and would also sit comfortably with its neighbours.

The RCP building is laid out on a T-shape design with an attached curved addition to the south, which houses a lecture theatre partly below ground level, and a circular meeting room to the north, added by Lasdun in the late 1990s. The primary part of the building consists of a bold, four-storey concrete block with a distinctive façade: the ground floor is clad in dark blue blocks and the remaining storeys in off-white mosaic tiles – a scheme that makes the upper levels appear as if they are floating. The top two levels, which contain the library and meeting and reception rooms, are supported by three slender columns on the entrance façade. Another distinctive feature is the windows – the top level has a series of narrow,

vertical, irregularly placed windows along its length, while the ground floor has a continuous band of glass – the variety greatly enlivens the façade. The building's flat roof is punctuated by two large, white towers, which house service areas. Leading at a right angle from this main block is a second four-storey building for offices.

In 1965, garden designer Mark Griffiths created a semi-sunken medicinal garden in the grounds, with each bed containing medicinal plants from a different part of the world. The College also owns an extensive collection of art and artefacts relating to medical history.

The influence of Le Corbusier (1887–1965) and Frank Lloyd Wright (1867–1959) are certainly apparent in the RCP headquarters, yet Lasdun's building also went on to greatly influence other architects (for example, mosaic-clad concrete became very popular in the 1960s). Although a controversial figure in his day, Lasdun also received much support and recognition for his work. The RCP is now largely viewed as one of the most important architectural statements of its time, and Lasdun was awarded the RIBA Gold Medal for Architecture in 1977.

Opposite: *The bold, Modernist form of the Royal College of Physicians is seen as one of the most important architectural statements of its time.* Above*: The square staircase winds up through the centre of the building, towards galleried floors above.*

The new Haberdashers' Hall, buried deep in the heart of the Smithfield area of east London, was opened in 2002 and was the first new Livery Hall to be built in the square mile that comprises the City of London for over 40 years. Livery companies are officially recognised trade associations – there are a total of 108 in the City – and many operate from a 'Hall' where business can be conducted and guests entertained. Designed by Michael Hopkins and Partners (see also pages 26, 66), this new building for the Haberdashers' Livery Company is a contemporary reinvention of historic precedent and tradition.

The Worshipful Company of Haberdashers (as it is also known) traces its long history to the 14th century. Originally, it was a fraternity formed by a group of City-based haberdashers who sold ribbons, beads, pins, purses, gloves and other small items and worshipped at St Paul's Cathedral; in 1502, they were joined by the hatmakers' fraternity. However, as London expanded, and it became impossible to regulate the haberdashery industry, the company gradually changed direction and became involved in charitable work. Today, the company supports schools in England and Wales and gives charitable grants for various worthwhile causes, primarily in the area of education but also for welfare, healthcare and churches; in addition, it continues to participate in the governance of the City of London.

The site for the new Haberdashers' Hall was a difficult one, as it was located in the middle of an urban block and therefore had no street frontage. The entrance leads under an old warehouse (now developed into residential apartments and retail units) and opens into an imposing but simple, two-storey cloistered courtyard

– a surprising pocket of tranquillity in the midst of this busy area of London. Most of the area is laid to grass, but one end of the quadrangle features a paved area, used for summer receptions and featuring a contemporary water feature by award-winning artist William Pye. Surrounding the courtyard is a two-storey, brick-built cloister of square arches, with a tall, pitched roof. The cloisters are part-open, like a loggia, and part-glazed, like a conservatory, creating a relaxed indoor–outdoor atmosphere and a more fluid sense of space.

Inside, a generously proportioned spiral staircase leads from the loggia to the first floor, which houses the formal ceremonial spaces. The Reception Gallery leads to the Courtroom, Committee Room and Luncheon Room, with the main Livery Hall at the far end. Hopkins treated this grand room – made almost entirely of wood (North American oak) – as a modern take on a medieval hall. The high-vaulted ceiling is of particular interest – the stainless-steel tracery is reminiscent of medieval beams, and its diagonal grid produces a strong, dynamic pattern that enlivens the space. On the ground floor are offices for staff, catering and storage areas, and accommodation for the Master and Beadle.

Hopkins' building reflects perfectly Haberdashers' ethos and ideals – an organisation that is contemporary and forward-thinking yet also respects history and tradition.

Above: The courtyard, with its distinctive square-arched cloister.
Opposite: The Livery Hall, panelled with North American oak, was designed as a modern take on a medieval hall.

LONDON AT HOME

'Inspiring, personal, interesting ... These houses show vision and give an idea of what architects can achieve by creating a model for new living both inside and outside.'
Open House London visitor

The London house, reflecting the personality and priorities of an individual or family, has always been a place of architectural innovation and experimentation – a place where architects can give expression to new ideas by realising a client's (or their own) personal vision. Leighton House is one of the best-known among historic examples in London, representing the unique mix of artist's studio and showcase, and luxurious place for entertaining, that its owner, leading Victorian artist Lord Leighton, wished to achieve. Ernö Goldfinger's 2 Willow Road, though on a smaller scale and in a more austere Modernist style, is a further evolution of this ideal.

Over the last 20 years, the house has been reinvented by contemporary architects to create new buildings that apply contemporary design solutions to questions of limited budget, reuse of existing structures, and maximising the amount of space available on severely restricted sites: the last an ever-increasing problem in London as almost every suitable site has already been built on. Brick House, Gap House, Ed's Shed, Quay House, and Whatcott's Yard all represent inventive responses to these issues.

With significant planning and other constraints on use of space, demand for housing in London has almost always exceeded supply. Following the devastation of World War II, the prime consideration for the government was to erect housing as quickly as possible, though it was still an issue in the 1970s when Trellick Tower was completed. Reflecting the architect's vision to create an exemplary housing model, this included community facilities such as a nursery and surgery. Today, this aim continues through mixed use developments that seek to combine community facilities and workspace alongside residences to create models for future sustainable communities. These not only encourage greener living – ever more important as London adapts to the effects of a changing climate – but also, often by looking at historic precedents such as Victorian terraces – seek to conceive new 'urban neighbourhoods'. As part of this, outside space is a carefully considered component of new and existing builds: external landscaped courtyards, balconies and roof gardens are frequently a feature of new urban developments. With London's demographics projected to change significantly in the next 20 years – with an extra one million inhabitants and a dramatic increase in the number of one-person households by 2030 – new design solutions will inevitably emerge to meet the changing needs of London's residents.

Leighton House, W14

In 1864, the eminent Victorian Classical painter Frederic Leighton (later 1st Baron Leighton) commissioned architect George Aitchison to build him a house just behind Kensington High Street, west London. The house was designed not only as a place in which Leighton could live and work, but as a social space in which he could entertain, and as a showcase for his substantial art collection. Construction began in 1866 and continued sporadically over the next 30 years as Leighton continued to extend his extraordinary home. To the artist, this building was both a work of art in its own right and was also deeply reflective of his important social standing – as well as being a respected artist, he was President of the Royal Academy between 1878 and 1896, and was the first painter ever to be given a peerage (although his hereditary Barony lasted for only one day, as he died the day after it was awarded).

From the building's simple, red-brick, classical-style exterior there are few clues to its remarkable interior, except possibly the rather grand domed octagon. Upon entering, however, the true nature of this spectacular studio–home, or 'private palace of art', as it is sometimes referred to, is revealed on the ground floor.

The centrepiece of Leighton House is the Arab Hall – a two-storey chamber that was added in 1877–79 to display Leighton's invaluable collection of over a thousand Islamic tiles (largely brought back from Syria), dating from the 14th to 17th centuries. Indeed, the entire space evokes a vision of the Middle East through its gold-painted, domed ceiling and carved wooden latticework windows, with further decoration from distinguished Victorian artists, including the golden mosaic frieze by Walter Crane and carved column capitals in the shape of exotic birds by Randolph Caldecott. Adding to the exotic character, at the centre of the hall stands a marble pool with a fountain, into which it is said some of Leighton's inebriated guests often tumbled to join the ornamental carp. Lining the walls of the passage that leads from the Arab Hall

are richly coloured, peacock-blue tiles by leading Victorian ceramicist and designer William de Morgan.

Leighton's extensive artist's studio is found on the first floor, complete with a dome, recess and ample north window. An impressive space, the studio was often used by Leighton for evening events, music recitals and entertaining, as well as for painting. For more intimate gatherings, Leighton would use the ground-floor dining room, with its rich-red floorboards, Islamic ceramics and Middle-Eastern artefacts. An avid collector, Leighton exhibited his treasures — many of which were the creations of his artist friends — throughout the house, including the Silk Room, which also doubled as a second studio space on the first floor. Despite the building's size and grandeur, it has only one bedroom, which was totally unadorned and stark in contrast to the rest of the house.

Leighton never married and had no heirs. On his death, the contents of the house were sold by his two sisters, but given its single bedroom and unusual layout it had little appeal as a domestic property and briefly became a children's library, with much of the décor being covered up. Later it became a museum, with many fine works of art on display, including Leighton's own paintings as well as those by George Frederick Watts, Sir Edward Burne-Jones, Sir John Everett Millais and other contemporaries in the Pre-Raphaelite Brotherhood.

Recent painstaking restoration by Purcell Miller Tritton (see also page 97), in 2010, has finally returned the property to its Victorian splendour, and won a 2011 RIBA London Award.

Opposite: *The simple red-brick exterior of Leighton House belies the opulent interior, the centrepiece of which is the Arab Hall* (above).

Left: *The building's façade is modelled on the style of 16th-century Italian villas.* Opposite: *The elegant staircase, with glass-domed roof letting in natural light.*

Built between 1762 and 1766, Danson House, in Bexleyheath, south-east London, is a rare survivor of an 18th-century building type once common in outer London – a rich City merchant's suburban villa or weekend retreat. It is modelled on 16ᵗʰ-century Italian villa design from the area around Vicenza and reflects the influence of the famous architect Andrea Palladio (1508–80).

The mansion was the product of the combined vision of Sir John Boyd – Vice Chairman of the British East India Company and son of a wealthy merchant with sugar plantations in the West Indies – and his architect Sir Robert Taylor. Taylor, who began his career as a statuary sculptor, built a number of town houses and villas for wealthy individuals including bankers, financiers, lawyers and directors of the East India Company, and was later known for his work on the Bank of England (see page 70). It is thought that renowned landscape architect Capability Brown and his assistant Nathaniel Richmond laid out the gardens.

A broad, graceful flight of steps leads to the grand entrance of the house. The façade is simple and elegantly proportioned, with an impressive doorway flanked with Corinthian columns, and a carved pediment featuring a round window providing the main decorative detail.

Inside, the stone entrance hall leads to an elliptical staircase around which all the rooms are ordered in a formal hierarchy, a compact form following Palladian principles. These include a grand dining room, where allegorical wall paintings by French artist Charles Pavillon depict romantic themes, inspired by Boyd's love for his new bride. There is also a dark green and mahogany library that contains the original Danson organ, which was made by the famous organ builder George England specifically for the house. The circuit of principal rooms culminates in the Octagonal Salon – the richest of the rooms, which required the most extensive restoration. The walls are covered in a delicate blue Chinoiserie-style paper, recreated to most closely match the original, while the white, gilded ceiling features eight distinct panels that radiate from a central rosette. The sweeping stairs leading up to the bedroom floor are top lit by a glass-topped dome and have a fine wrought-iron balustrade.

The house was auctioned by Boyd's son in 1805 and bought by businessman John Johnston, who added an orangery to the landscaped gardens and a Gothic-style cottage in the grounds. Watercolours of the house and its interiors by Johnston's daughter, Sarah, from 1860, proved invaluable during the restoration work, and the interiors have now been recreated in their original form.

In 1862, Danson House was bought

by railway engineer and Chairman of the Bexley Heath Railway project, Alfred Bean, who refurbished the interior in an Imperial French Rococo style and updated it with gas lighting and hot water. After the deaths of Alfred and his widow, Bexley Council bought the house, in 1923. The grounds, including the garden, were opened as a public park, managed by the council, and the house became a museum.

In 1995, English Heritage considered the site to be 'the most significant building at risk' in London, and bought the site on a long lease to carry out the extensive repairs and restoration needed. It commissioned architects Purcell Miller Tritton (see also page 95) to undertake an extensive and sympathetic restoration that returned this Georgian mansion to its former splendour by 2004. The lease was assigned to Bexley Heritage Trust, and the newly renovated house was formally opened in 2005. In 2006, Danson Park was restored with support from the Heritage Lottery Fund.

2 Willow Road, NW3

Designed by the Hungarian-born architect Ernö Goldfinger (see also pages 102–103) for his family to live in, 2 Willow Road was both a domestic haven and a richly artistic, creative space. Built in 1939, the house is a rare and superbly preserved example of early Modern architecture that has remained virtually untouched since the family lived there. It was acquired by the National Trust in 1994 and still contains its original furniture and fittings, largely designed by the architect and his daughter, Elizabeth.

Goldfinger encountered difficulties in gaining planning consent for his proposed home on a site overlooking Hampstead Heath. Construction of the new buildings required demolition of a number of cottages, and was strongly opposed by several local residents, including the novelist Ian Fleming (it is said that the James Bond villain Auric Goldfinger is named after the architect). Finally, plans were accepted for a terrace of three houses, with a large central house for the architect flanked by two smaller properties. The terraced configuration, simple repetitive geometry of the design and red-brick façade (as opposed to a concrete façade, which was a feature of Continental Modernism – though used by Goldfinger in his later work) recognised the precedent of surrounding Georgian properties, helping to appease local opposition. However, the basic structure is a reinforced concrete frame that allows a freedom of layout and much larger windows than is possible with conventional load-bearing walls.

Externally, the building has a symmetrical rhythm achieved through the window placement and simple architectural detail. The first-floor windows of the house provide a continuous band of glass that allows natural light into the interior living rooms, while on the second floor, which houses the bedrooms, the windows are considerably smaller with white frames.

It is the interior, though, that really defines this building and reflects the skill of Goldfinger as both architect and designer in his manipulation of living space and his attention to detail. He was an early advocate of open-plan living, and incorporated a series of sliding and folding partitions that could be used to alter the size or function of the interior spaces. Entrance to the house is through a simple doorway that leads into the ground floor, which contains the service areas, including the garage and kitchen. At the end of the hall is an elegant spiral staircase featuring concrete stairs and a brass handrail, which immediately sets the character of the interior. Light, simplicity and various complementary textures are key elements of the overall design, as are space-saving devices such as built-in cupboards.

Ernö and his wife Ursula were avid collectors of modern art, and pieces by Marcel Duchamp, Max Ernst, Henry Moore and Bridget Riley, among others, are still in situ. Influenced by Le Corbusier (1887–1965) and Cubist painters, the architect used colour throughout on the walls and floors to create different moods, which become lighter and brighter progressing upwards through the house.

In 2 Willow Road, Goldfinger created a small pocket of cohesive Modernism – a building that was controversial in its day, but was ultimately of significant influence in the burgeoning new architectural movement in the United Kingdom.

Above: *The simple architectural detail of the exterior hints at the distinctively modern interior* (opposite), *dominated by Goldfinger's skilful use of space, light and texture.*

The Beddington Zero Energy Development (BedZED) is a large, mixed-use development that set new standards in sustainable building when completed in 2002. Located in Sutton, a south London borough, it is the biggest carbon-neutral, mixed-use scheme in the United Kingdom and has become a model for sustainable community developments.

BedZED was developed by Bill Dunster Architects in association with Peabody, one of London's oldest and largest housing associations (founded in 1862), and environmental consultants BioRegional Development Group. The aim behind the design concept was to create a development that produces at least as much energy from renewable sources as it consumes. Built on the site of a former sewage works, the development includes 82 residential dwellings (flats, maisonettes and town houses), plus workspaces, an exhibition centre, a children's nursery and a showflat.

The combination of privately owned, shared ownership and social housing means that BedZED is home to a mixed community. However, elements of the design encourage both sustainability and a sense of community spirit. The buildings are constructed as far as possible from eco-friendly materials, with emphasis placed on obtaining materials from within an 80-kilometre (50-mile) radius of the site to ensure carbon emissions are kept to a minimum. The houses are arranged in five separate, south-facing terraces. All are three storeys high, have conservatories to maximise heat gain from the sun, and benefit from large windows to make the

best use of natural light. Each terrace is backed by north-facing offices, where minimal solar gain reduces overheating and the need for air conditioning.

The houses promote a greener lifestyle through the incorporation of numerous measures, such as low-energy appliances, multi-recycling bins, double-flush lavatories and low-flow showers. The scheme also involves rainwater harvesting, a combined heat and power plant, photovoltaic panels and natural wind-driven ventilation – the latter accounting for the colourful roof cowls that announce the development's unique character from a distance. Electricity is provided to charge electric cars, although residents are encouraged to join 'car pools' and to either walk, cycle or use public transport. The car-parking spaces are located at the perimeters of the site, leaving large areas in the centre free for pedestrians, making it a safer environment for children.

All the houses have gardens or roof terraces, created on top of the workspaces, with some accessed via bridges that connect buildings together. In addition, the site provides community vegetable plots, which as well as enabling residents to grow their own food encourages people to interact with one another. The community-focused design of BedZed seems to have been very successful – a survey undertaken at the development in 2004 indicated that residents were familiar with at least 20 of their neighbours, in contrast to other urban areas where the average figure is nearer eight. The project was also shortlisted for the RIBA Stirling Prize in 2003.

Opposite: *BedZED's colourful roof cowls are not merely decorative – they are a mechanism for wind-driven ventilation in this model sustainable development. It includes 82 residential dwellings* (above).

The 31-storey Trellick Tower in North Kensington, west London, was designed by the Hungarian-born architect Ernö Goldfinger (see also page 98) and built between 1968 and 1973. For some years it was the tallest block of flats in England. A controversial building, it was commissioned by the Greater London Council, which was still trying to counteract the effects of massive housing demolition during World War II through tower-block construction. Lack of council money to fund security and maintenance led to the building becoming dilapidated and a crime spot during the late 1970s and early 1980s, at a time when high-rise Modernist tower blocks were becoming increasingly unpopular. In the mid-1980s, the occupants formed a residents' association to put pressure on the council

to improve security; since then, a door-entry intercom system and CCTV have been installed, and a concierge employed. Trellick Tower's image has changed; while the flats continue to be primarily social housing a number are privately owned, and today the block is considered by many as a desirable residence.

By the time of the Trellick commission, Goldfinger had already built the 27-storey Balfron Tower (1965–67) in Tower Hamlets. After completing Balfron, Goldfinger and his wife, Ursula, moved into one of the flats for two months so he could meet the other residents and discover how well the building functioned. He invited his neighbours to an evening cocktail party at his flat, where he encouraged them to reveal their likes and dislikes about living in the tower, and took these comments into account when designing Trellick in an attempt to create the perfect social housing model.

With its simple, stark form and raw use of materials (primarily concrete), Trellick Tower reflects Goldfinger's Brutalist style. It is designed as two linked blocks, one housing flats and maisonettes (217 in total), and the second, much slimmer tower containing the lifts and services. The projection at the top is the plant room, which is now redundant but originally housed the boiler and hot-water tanks.

The two towers are linked every three storeys by covered walkways, with the floors above and below the corridors in the residential block accessed by internal staircases. As well as serving a practical function, these walkways add to the symmetry and rhythm of the building's visual aspect. Dividing up the façade with great regularity are balconies and large windows, which allow as much natural light in as possible and provide excellent

views. The original interiors demonstrated Goldfinger's clever space-saving designs, such as sliding doors, and actually provided a larger floor space than was typical of social housing of the time. The architect's attention to detailing is evident in such features as the cedar boarding of the balconies, the low swivel windows for ease of cleaning, and light switches fitted into the door frames.

Reflecting Goldfinger's vision of architecture as a vehicle for social organisation, Trellick Tower was designed with its own nursery school, doctor's surgery, old people's club, laundrette and shops; the architect also wanted to have a pub on site, but eventually he moved his office into the designated space and worked there for the last five years of his career. This form of all-inclusive living, with public facilities set alongside residential units, was loosely modelled on Le Corbusier's famous Unité d'Habitation in Marseille (1947–52), which had influenced the Brutalist architectural style and philosophy.

Opposite: *This instantly recognizable Brutalist structure in West London was an attempt by Goldfinger to create the perfect social housing model.*
Above: *Balconies and large windows provide excellent views and allow in as much natural light as possible.*

Adelaide Wharf, E2

The vibrant Adelaide Wharf development, built alongside the Regent's Canal on the site of an old timber wharf, is an important part of the regeneration of this area of Hackney, east London. Finished in 2011, the scheme was part of the London-Wide Initiative in collaboration with English Partnerships (now Homes and Communities Agency) to produce high-quality, sustainable homes at affordable prices, with communal facilities for all residents. Commissioned by urban developer First Base and designed by Allford Hall Monaghan Morris (see also pages 14, 152, 160), it consists of 147 new flats divided between privately owned, shared ownership and social housing, plus an additional 650 square metres (almost 7,000 square feet) of workspace that has been assigned to a community-run regeneration agency, the Shoreditch Trust. All the homes are built to the same high specification, regardless of whether they are privately owned, shared ownership or social housing.

The architects worked closely with construction specialists Bovis Lend Lease to develop ultra-efficient methods to reduce the build time and keep costs to a minimum; these included the use of prefabricated elements, such

as the bathroom pods, balconies and preassembled cladding, which negated the need for scaffolding. The resulting systems were so effective that they are now a model for this type of building.

Adelaide Wharf is a six-storey block that wraps around three sides of a landscaped courtyard, with the canal bordering the fourth side. This central open space is crucial to the building's design, providing the residents with a quiet, safe sanctuary in a busy urban area. The emphasis on outside space is further evident in the large balconies, which provide an outdoor 'room' and excellent views over the canal,

courtyard or street below. Forming an important part of the building's aesthetics, the warm-coloured balconies, in red, pink, yellow and orange, contrast with the rest of the façade, which is composed of layers of roughly sawn larch, reminiscent of the wooden packing crates that used to be stored on this site.

Welcoming visitors and residents to the building are two entrances made from brightly coloured, vitreous enamel panels and glass, offering glimpses to the courtyard beyond. Inside the block, the main entrance lobby and stairs are lined with a 16-metre (52-foot) tall wooden art installation by local artist Richard Woods, which again acts as a reminder of the site's former connection with timber. The apartments are spacious and largely open plan, with all the service areas placed along the corridor wall. The living and sleeping spaces have floor-to-ceiling windows, and the one-bedroom apartments have double doors between the living and sleeping areas, which can be opened to create a sense of space or closed for privacy.

The building's architectural merit is reflected in a number of prizes, including the Hackney Design Award, 2008, and a RIBA National Award, 2008.

Above: *Colourful balconies and spacious, predominantly open-plan apartments* (opposite) *disguise the cost- and time-effective construction of the building.*

The housing development at Claredale Street is the first phase of an extensive regeneration programme of the Mansford Estates in a deprived part of Bethnal Green, east London – an area that consisted of a disparate collection of 1960s high- and low-rise tower blocks, Victorian terraces and poorly planned public thoroughfares. Completed in 2010, the development was designed by Karakusevic Carson Architects in close collaboration with Tower Hamlets Community Housing, London Borough of Tower Hamlets, English Heritage and, importantly, with a local residents group, which defined the requirements and aspirations of the local community. The aim was to replace a high-rise modern block (Bradley House) and re-establish a range of housing types from flats to two-, three- or four-bedroom homes on the scale and pattern of the Victorian terraces that once characterised the area.

The Claredale Street development features three main elements – a principal apartment block, individual town houses and a terrace block containing courtyard flats and maisonettes. Conceived as an urban courtyard, it has a pedestrian-friendly route through the middle (Teesdale Street), which provides access to landscaped areas. The architects sought to create a 'mini-neighbourhood', providing a safe, cheerful environment to inspire pride

among the residents, with a combination of shared courts, private gardens and houses that open directly onto the street to create a sociable feel. A total of 77 new homes have been created, including 40 per cent affordable housing. The accommodation is varied and takes account of a mix of privately owned homes and social housing, and caters to people of all ages, from families with young children to the over-60s.

The apartment block, which is seven storeys high and has an animated façade of irregular balconies, is divided into studios and one- to three-bedroom flats. The top floor contains a series of penthouses with views. Behind the apartment block, at the western edge of the site, are two- or three-storey town houses, with gardens or terraces behind. At the east end of the site is a three-storey terrace block, which is cleverly designed to look like a row of town houses but is in fact divided into a series of ground-floor flats with maisonettes on the top two floors of the block. The flats extend the width of the building and open onto a private glazed courtyard at the back, while the maisonettes have a rear terrace on the second storey as well as a recessed balcony overlooking the street.

The scheme aims to achieve high standards of energy saving. All the buildings in the development have photovoltaic panels on green roofs to heat hot water and are faced in copper sheet, which is fixed with an irregular pattern of joints to give it a 'handmade' look. The copper cladding adds warmth and texture to the buildings.

The success of the Claredale Street housing development has been recognised with a large number of prestigious awards, including the Richard Feilden Award for Housing in the Housing Design Awards, 2010, and a RIBA London Award, 2011.

Above: *Claredale Street echoes Victorian terraces in its scale and pattern.*
Opposite: *The flats extend the width of each building and open onto private courtyards.*

1–3 Whatcott's Yard, N16

Whatcott's Yard – an unusual new-build housing project – sits on a long, narrow site tucked away between the back gardens of two Victorian terraces in Stoke Newington, north-east London (hence the development's alternative name, the In-Between). It was the brainchild of three friends – architects Annalie Riches and Silvia Ullmayer and designer Barti Garibaldo – who decided to design and build their own properties to live in, sharing the costs. As such, it is a prime example of how young professionals can create innovative solutions on a very limited budget. Together, they bought the former industrial site and set about designing a simple, light building that would nevertheless enable each of them to design their own home according to their individual requirements. At the same time, they aimed to create three houses of equal footprint, volume and orientation, reflecting the essence of the surrounding Victorian terraces. They produced a highly cost- and time-effective plan, and each took a year off work between 2001 and 2004 in order to concentrate on the project.

The terrace is divided into three equal parts, each with an area of just 45 square metres (484 square feet), and consists of two houses with the third dwelling now divided into two flats. The materials used were low cost and often recycled or from renewable sources. The main construction material is reconstituted timber, insulation is provided by a combination of recycled newspaper and sheep's wool, and each has a green roof. The south wall of the houses is completely transparent, with glazing made from a combination of lightweight polycarbonate sheeting and glass, and each of the three dwellings opens onto a small terrace. As a result, all the interiors feel light and spacious and strongly connected with the outside.

The development has won a number of awards, including the AJ First Building Award and RIBA Award (both 2004), and is an inspiration to those wanting to turn a small area into a highly liveable home.

Above: *The fully glazed south wall increases the feeling of light and space inside this unusual housing project.*

Left: *Each home has been designed according to the individual architect's requirements.*

Quay House is a live/work space that is the product of architect Ken Taylor and artist Julia Manheim's creative vision and is a great example of reuse of an existing derelict building and recycling of materials. The former industrial building used to be a dairy, probably built during the late 1930s. By 1998, when Taylor first saw the property, it was owned by the coucil. Recognising the potential of the building to provide space for a workshop, studio, gallery, office and living area, Taylor and Manheim bought it and set about an innovative rebuild, which was undertaken in two phases and completed in 2002.

The owners converted the back half of the property and some dilapidated outbuildings at the rear into private living spaces, with a kitchen and small library taking the place of the original cold store, which used to house the milk churns. They were keen to retain as much of the industrial 'urban barn' character and the building's history as possible, so they stripped the kitchen floors back to their

Right: *A view from the street of this distinctive multi-use building.*
Below: *Colourful, textured materials create an uplifting environment.*

industrial base and painted them silver. The internal doors are reused from the original building, except fire doors, giving better thermal performance. Upstairs, above the cold store, are three bedrooms and a bathroom in the form of beach huts, clad in western red cedar boarding.

The front half of the building (where both architect and artist lived throughout the construction process) contains the more public spaces: two mini-galleries and studio space for Manheim and Quay 2c – Taylor's multidisciplinary firm of architects, designers and artists. Above are three new-build, loft-style separate flats with their own entrance and staircase.

The interior space in this contemporary multi-use building is cohesively simple and effective, with colour and textured materials creating the distinctive visual aesthetic and a light, uplifting feel.

Burton House, NW5

Built in 1987 (studio 1990 and annex 2002) by architect Richard Burton, of Ahrends Burton Koralek Architects, Burton House is an acutely innovative piece of contemporary architecture that balances energy conservation with liveability. Burton and his architect partners, Peter Ahrends and Paul Koralek – well known for a number of their buildings including the British Embassy in Moscow – have had a long, close relationship with the development of English Modernism in architecture. It was Burton's grandmother who commissioned Modernist architect F. R. S. Yorke (author of *The Modern House* in 1934) to design his first house Torilla, in Hertfordshire, which is now considered an important exemplar of 1930s domestic architecture.

Burton found an end-of-terrace site in Kentish Town, north-west London, that had not yet been developed on which to build a home for himself and his wife to live in. The building, which is set against the northern side of the site boundary and

faces south to maximise heat from the sun in winter and keep well-shaded in summer, is arranged around a courtyard garden that provides a very private and secure outside space at the heart of this small complex.

The visitor enters the property through an intriguing doorway, which gives a clue to the inspiring building that lies behind the high brick wall exterior. A large, circular gate with wavy vertical bands of undulating steel, it has all the presence of a fortified portal, beyond which is a porch in which grows a magnificent 150-year-old plane tree.

The front door of the building opens into a long, glass-covered entrance hall, or

conservatory, which is south-facing and allows light to flood through the glazing, making the house feel more spacious than it actually is and bringing the outside into the building. There are three rooms off the hall – the kitchen/dining room, living room and Mrs Burton's study, and a staircase leads to a bedroom upstairs. Large sliding doors open from these rooms onto the hallway or conservatory, so that the central space can also become an extension to these rooms. On the other side of the conservatory, further accommodation is provided in the form of a garden studio, so the architect can work at home, and an annexe for the Burton's daughter. In all,

this is an effective grouping of separate areas that provides for private, individual space as well as sociable, communal areas.

Highly effective insulation is used throughout the house to improve energy efficiency. It has photovoltaic panels and a solar water heating system. The annexe has a green roof and is mainly built of timber and brick. Art and craft works abound.

Burton House – a self-built property with much involvement by the family – is an uplifting domestic residence that matches supreme quality of design, execution and materials with an inspiring plan that accounts for the specific needs of the family: a country house in the city.

Opposite: *The long conservatory/ hall looks out on to a courtyard garden* (left), *and has three rooms leading off it, including the living room* (above).

d's Shed, also known as the Sunken House, is a prime example of contemporary minimalism that was built in record time in 2007 over a few days and was completely finished inside and out within roughly ten months. From the outside, there is little to indicate that this black wooden box is a house: simply a plain slot window at the front. However, inside the building is characterised by simple shapes and forms, clean lines, tremendous use of light and great attention to the manipulation of space.

The house was commissioned by photographer Ed Reeve and designed by architect David Adjaye, who met in the 1990s. They decided to collaborate on a simple, low-maintenance residential property and spent some years searching for the ideal site in London, at an affordable price. The plot, in a conservation area of Hackney, north-east London, eventually came up for sale, providing the perfect opportunity for their plans to be realised. The rapid construction of the house was due to its largely prefabricated nature – engineered by building contractors Eurban Construction, it was built off site and assembled *in situ*.

To create the maximum amount of space in this small plot, Adjaye designed the house to have a lower-ground level floor, or basement, which leads onto a sunken courtyard (hence the building's name). The entrance to the house is at ground level and passes over the roof of the lower-ground floor. The front door is carefully concealed within the wood cladding of the exterior and is barely visible – there is no door furniture, just a hole for the key. This allows the entire exterior to appear as if it were covered in a continuous unbroken 'skin' of dark-stained cedar cladding, which seems to envelop the structure. This

cladding extends to the ground surface of the concrete patio, so there is unbroken continuity through the vertical and horizontal aspects.

Inside the house, the dark grey, pale blue and white colour scheme, designed by Elizabeth Macleod, Reeve's sister, works seamlessly with the dark exterior and the minimal nature of the building. The entrance-level floor contains a bedroom, office and utility room, while the lower-ground floor houses the large, open-plan kitchen/diner leading on to the courtyard, a bathroom and a second bedroom. The top floor provides the living space and is painted brilliant white for a clean, simple, modern look. A large 'picture' window seems to frame views of the trees outside – which initially attracted Ed Reeve to this site – and allows daylight to flood in and reflect on the white resin floor, adding to the vibrant feel of this minimalist interior. Hidden behind a wall of cabinets is a small balcony, which many visitors to the house are unaware of. Indeed, concealment and

surprise is a continuing theme within the house: only one of the windows opens, with the rest of the ventilation provided by opening panels that appear to form part of the walls; there is even a trapdoor in the ceiling of the living space, with a pull-down ladder that leads to the roof and provides another unusual outdoor space with views.

Ed's Shed is full of surprises – there is a sense of adventure that begins with finding the front door and continues through to the interiors, which are full of unexpected spaces and light. This refined yet minimal design also uses environmentally friendly materials: hemp insulation improves the thermal performance of the structure, while the solid timber frame provides a significantly reduced carbon footprint.

Opposite: *The building looks more like a black wooden box from the outside than a house and the interiors continue the minimalist theme with clean lines* (left) *and a large picture window framing external views* (above).

Gap House – designed by Luke Tozer of Pitman Tozer Architects and completed in 2007 – is a phenomenal achievement in terms of manipulation of a difficult site to create a comfortable, environmentally friendly home for himself and his family.

As its name implies, the house fills a narrow gap, just 2.3 metres (8 feet) wide, between two listed buildings in a conservation area of Bayswater, west London. This slender space widens towards the back, where there was originally a dilapidated cottage and a small garden. The architect has described entering his home as being akin to the children's television programme *Mr Benn*, where the character enters a tiny changing room in a fancy-dress costume shop and is whisked into a whole new, magical world. Behind the narrow façade, Tozer has created a home that feels remarkably spacious and light.

From the outside, the slender white building is fairly inconspicuous, with the height and spacing of its windows responding to those of the elegant buildings on either side, but on entering through the front door the full contemporary character of this comfortable home prevails.

The narrow entrance hall opens into a kitchen/diner, which leads to a surprisingly large living space that wraps around a courtyard garden at the back. A sliding glass wall separates the inside from the outside, drawing light into the living area and making the space feel larger; to further enhance the feeling of being outdoors, the wall can be opened completely. The seamless transition from outside to inside is reinforced by the continuous floor from the courtyard to the kitchen/living area. Above, the master bedroom looks down onto the courtyard.

Tozer located his children's bedrooms at the front of the house – where noise would be kept at a distance from the living areas – placing them one room on top of the other in identical-sized spaces. A central void with a roof light above the stairs allows daylight to flood the interior.

The building also has exceptional green credentials – it was a finalist in Channel 4's *Grand Designs*' Eco House of the Year 2008, while its design excellence was further recognised by the award of the RIBA Manser Medal in 2009. The residence uses approximately one third of the energy of a new house built to current building regulations. To reduce energy consumption, it is highly insulated and heating is provided through geothermal sources. Rainwater is harvested to flush the lavatories. Materials from sustainable sources were also used where possible.

The ecological efficiency all takes place quietly in the background, but what is immediately evident is that this is a warm, contemporary home that combines child-friendly living with sophistication.

Right: *Gap House subverts the expectations generated by its exceptionally slim façade, widening out at the back to create a spacious home* (opposite).

Brick House, completed in 2005, is a contemporary family home that has been fashioned from an almost impossible site by Caruso St John Architects. Caruso St John were approached some years ago by clients who expressed a desire to live in their own custom-designed home in this fashionable quarter of west London – an area where building plots are virtually non-existent. The architects searched for a suitable site throughout 2001, before happening on a small, horseshoe-shaped plot surrounded by Victorian, Edwardian and 1960s buildings at the end of a cul-de-sac. The client's brief was extremely challenging, but Caruso St John met and matched the problems to create a unique town house suitable for the family to live in.

As its name suggests, the house is built almost entirely from brick – a fairly unfashionable material in current times (especially for internal finishes), when concrete and glass tend to predominate, but one that works extremely well given the building's context. On a practical level, bricks afforded the architects the easiest build solution on a site where extensive concrete work was not possible because there was insufficient space to install a crane. From an aesthetic point of view, the cohesive use of brick both inside and outside creates a warm, textured effect. Red bricks are used on the exterior, while the interior features soft-yellow bricks, which are left exposed to create a simple, patterned look.

The shape of the site has determined the form of the living space. Rather than encouraging interaction with the outside, as is the case when glass predominates (and which would have been inappropriate for a site that is so overlooked), the design focuses inwards and is almost cave-like in

its conception. The house rises only one floor above street level, and has a lower-ground floor, or basement, so the space feels private and enclosed.

From the street, there is little indication of the house's existence – the entrance is through an arch in the existing Victorian terrace and there is no visible façade. However, beyond the arch a long, broad ramp rises from street level and leads towards the front door and, surprisingly, the ramp continues and leads gently into the spacious living area. Dominating this living space is a massive polished concrete ceiling, which had to be cast on site. It varies in height throughout the space, being lower over the dining area and higher over the living area, and is punctuated by carefully placed roof lights, which funnel natural light into the interior in striking patterns. The complex nature of this ceiling, with its combination of angles and openings, creates a dramatic atmosphere for the social part of the house.

Quite different in character from the living areas are the bedrooms, all of which are located in the basement. With their low ceilings and small size, these rooms feel safe, peaceful and intimate – a haven from the outside world. The glass walls, which offer views onto three, brick-lined external courtyards, increase the sense of space in the rooms, preventing them from feeling oppressive, and lend an air of elegance.

The house is infused with a quiet grandeur, achieved through the continuous and sophisticated brickwork, the manipulation of natural light and the sculptural feel to the inside of the building. As a mark of its success, Brick House has won a number of prestigious awards, including a RIBA London Award, 2006, and it was shortlisted for the RIBA Stirling Prize in the same year.

Opposite: With only one floor above ground level, the building feels discreet and enclosed. Overleaf: Carefully placed roof lights funnel natural light into the rooms in striking patterns (here the kitchen).

Named for their location at one of the highest points in London, apartment blocks Highpoint I and Highpoint II are the work of architect Berthold Lubetkin and structural engineer Ove Arup.

Entrepreneur Sigmund Gestetner commissioned Highpoint with the initial intention of providing housing for the workers at his company, and although it was never in fact used for this purpose the building was clearly designed to respond to the growing need for innovative, compact spaces for urban living.

Highpoint I, which was completed in 1935, comprises two cruciform towers, housing 64 two- and three-bedroom flats. The building unfolds as you walk through it: the entrance, at ground floor level, with its white pilotis, leads onto a shared reception area and to other communal spaces such as the winter garden and terrace. Two lifts service the two towers and a common roof.

While largely influenced by and conforming to the standards of Le Corbusier, Highpoint is notable for its many technical innovations: advances in construction included having the walls and floors built out of a single block to reduce problems with structural cracks, and the concrete walls were made using removable platforms preventing the need for scaffolding; technological modernisations saw the use of communal heating and refrigeration systems; design innovations included built-in wardrobes and fridges as well as services lifts to and from the kitchen or hallway.

The advanced functionality of Highpoint did not mean that aesthetics were compromised. The building is a prime example of the International style. Its white façade has become a landmark of the area, with its cantilevered balconies, and concertina windows which were intended to open as much living space as possible to the outside.

Lubetkin convinced Gestetner to buy land to the south of Highpoint I where he subsequently constructed Highpoint II in 1938. Highpoint had, however,

caused some controversy with the local community, resulting in the establishment of the Highgate Preservation Committee, which insisted that any future construction had to conform to the architectural character of the area.

As a consequence, Highpoint II became limited to a fifth of the size of the original, and instead of housing 57 flats, the building became a block of 12 luxury maisonettes. While it shared a number of features with Highpoint I, including having two connected towers with a common reception area and roof terrace, this was built over a traditional concrete frame.

Highpoint represents the evolutionary peak of Lubetkin's work, and so it is fitting that he built himself a penthouse apartment at the top of Highpoint II where he lived until 1955.

Above: *The penthouse of Highpoint II, which Lubetkin built for his own occupation.*
Opposite: *The cruciform buildings of Highpoint I.*
Left: *Distinctive white pilotis distinguish the entrance to Highpoint I.*

The glass-and-cedar-clad Berresford House was built in 1957–58 by architect Ivor Berresford, for himself and his wife to live in. It represents the work of the architect at the start of his long career, when he was experimenting with forms and ideas, free from the restraints of working for a client. The house occupies a sloping site surrounded by trees in the suburb of Bromley, south-east London, in a location that balances urban living with a quiet, almost rural feel. Berresford specifically wanted a setting and house that would be suitable for what he hoped would be a growing family, and he purchased the site and constructed the timber-framed building for £6,350 (the average price for a house in the United Kingdom was £2,500 by the end of the 1950s).

The architect's design was both forward thinking for the times and also sympathetic to the location – he managed to strike a balance between creating a dynamic and impressive modern home while also designing it to complement rather than contrast with its site. With its flat roof, the two-storey house has a low profile and is set back into the sloping site. The ground floor is a dark brick, while the top storey is defined by cedar cladding, which echoes the wooded nature of the surroundings.

The three bedrooms and bathroom are, unusually for a family home, on the ground floor, as is the garage. The beauty of the interior lies in its 'raw' decoration – for example, the hallway has walls that are left unplastered and leads to an open-tread staircase with a natural hardwood handrail. In the main bedrooms, one complete wall consists of sliding panels, concealing all the storage areas – hanging space, drawers and dressing table.

All the main rooms are on the first floor, including the open-plan living room. One wall is entirely clad in glass, and sliding doors open out onto a generous decked

area, which leads onto the sloping garden beyond and creates an effective crossover of indoor and outdoor space. Continuing the use of natural materials, the ceiling is covered in pine, which again creates a link with the trees outside.

When it was built, the house was viewed as quite a radical, post-war modern building. Today, although it remains 1960s in feel, there is also something strikingly contemporary about it that fits neatly with

current tastes. The simple minimalism continues to be appreciated, and many of the original fixtures and fittings have remained unchanged in the house. Indeed, its authenticity has made it a popular filming location for fashion shoots and music videos for bands, including the British group Blur. In 2008 – over 50 years after its construction – it was dubbed 'the perfect house' by the television programme *Grand Designs*.

Above: *Pine-covered ceilings create a natural link to the garden beyond the living room.*
Opposite: *Sliding glass doors increase the sense of immediacy between the interior and exterior, and lead on to a decked area.*

When a mews workshop at the end of artist Philip Hughes' garden in Kentish Town came on the market, the ideal opportunity arose for him to convert the run-down property into an art studio and exhibition space for his works and collections, with the rather unusual addition of a home spa. His aim was to create a space in a dense urban setting that would reflect creativity and imagination, provoke thought and be a place of sensory stimulation, and he named the building Artchive.

Hughes enlisted his daughter, Francesca, and her American partner, Jonathon Meyer, to design the rebuild of the mews, which took place between 2003 and 2005. Their practice, Hughes Meyer Studio, collaborated on the project with friends Abigail Hopkins and Amir Sanei of Sanei Hopkins Architects. For Francesca, the project was intensely personal, as she had grown up in the Victorian house that overlooks the garden and mews building.

The basic shell of the mews workshop was retained, including its relatively blank street façade, which accommodates the studio's entrance and gives little indication of the extraordinary space within. However, at the back of the building the architects added a two-storey extension, using a variety of ingenious methods to make the space feel larger and more dynamic, largely through their use of mirrors and glass.

The extension (engineered by Matthew Wells from Techniker) has a 45-degree pitched roof that echoes the angle of the roofs around it, but due to its glass construction it is rendered almost transparent. The roof flattens out over the top of the single-storey part of the extension, which is clad internally and externally in mirrors that reflect the garden, the sky and the workshop, creating an illusion of extended and surreal space. Not only does this magical glass/mirror extension create great visual impact within the garden, it is also fascinating to see from the perspective of the artist's existing house, with the art works in the mews 'on view' for those looking from the upper

windows. Francesca says of the building, 'Spatially there is not that much going on, optically it is much more complex.'

Within the converted mews workshop are two freestanding sculptural forms that contain the spa elements of the design – a mirrored box and an irregular-shaped, ceramic-tiled structure that house the sauna and steam room respectively.

This is an inspired small-building project and is a result of close and personal collaboration. It brings together the idiosyncratic requirements of the client and manages to convey them with a brilliant originality.

Above: *The architects made ingenious use of mirrors and glass to make the space feel larger.*

Wrap House, W4

Wrap House, designed by Alison Brooks Architects and completed in 2005, consists of a highly unusual extension creating a complex set of spaces in the garden of an existing Edwardian family home in west London. The brief was to create additional space on the ground floor, which would be a single open-plan area for a variety of different uses. A further requirement was that the extension should be as exciting to look at from above as from ground level, because the master bedroom of the main building would overlook it.

To this end, Brooks devised a single-storey structure that is unified through its mellow wood cladding, which covers the building like a 'skin' (hence the name Wrap House) and extends to create a variety of linked and continuous spaces, then spills out into the garden, forming a deck and storage area all covered in the same material. The extension attaches to the existing house through a glass-covered 'linking' area, which announces the separate character of this structure and allows natural light to flood into the interior. Looked at from above, the glazed strip and wood cladding fit into the garden landscape, and the roof is structured so that views of the garden from the master bedroom are not restricted.

The walls of the angular extension are covered largely in glass, which allows light through and creates a sense of space; it also makes a visual connection between the interior and exterior areas – the garden and in particular the deck appear as a projection of the extension. Jutting from the end wall of the room, the deck has an organic feel and wraps around a large, existing tree. To one side, the roof cladding 'folds' down and out to create a simple storage and barbecue area to one side of the house.

Inside, the space is flooded with light, creating an uplifting atmosphere. The interior walls and ceiling are painted white, and the strongly sculptural ceiling matches the exterior roofline. These triangulated geometric shapes across the ceiling – the most distinctive part of the design – create the illusion of individual areas within the large room. The overall appearance of the room is one of great simplicity, and belies the underlying sophistication of the design.

Left: *The clean, simple shapes of the interior mask the underlying sophistication of the design.*

Wrap House is a clear demonstration of one of Alison Brooks's principal aims – namely, the creation of buildings that people enjoy living in, or 'happy' spaces. As a mark of its imaginative design, Wrap House won the RIBA Stephen Lawrence Award, 2006, and was also shortlisted for the RIBA Manser Medal in the same year.

Right: *The building is 'wrapped' in a mellow wood cladding.*

Situated in the suburb of Wimbledon, south-west London, 31B St Mary's Road is one of several modest private homes designed by the architects Peter Foggo and David Thomas, who studied together in Liverpool. Between 1959 and 1965, the two friends, who at the time worked together as Peter Foggo David Thomas Architects, designed a number of private residences that are notable for the purity and simplicity of their form and the manner in which they integrate into their surroundings while still making a bold modern statement. Later, both Foggo and Thomas became directors of Arup Associates before Foggo formed Foggo Associates in 1989.

31B St Mary's Road was finished in 1965 and is one of a series of three houses, initially identical, built in the grounds of a large Edwardian house. 31B is the only one to retain virtually all the original features, including the matching car port and interior room layout. Both houses reveal the influence of the American Case Study Houses scheme, which was a post-World War II building project in which major architects, such as Richard Neutra and Craig Ellwood, were commissioned to design and build efficient, inexpensive, inspiring homes to cater to the residential housing boom of 1945 to the mid-1960s. The Case Study project was sponsored by *Arts and Architecture* magazine, with the underlying aim being to encourage stimulating and attractive designs for low-budget homes.

31B St Mary's Road most clearly recalls Farnsworth House near Plano in Illinois, USA, which was designed by German architect and pioneer of the Modern movement, Ludwig Mies van der Rohe (1886–1969). Built in 1951, Farnsworth House is a Modern landmark building

that represents architecture distilled to its absolute essential parts, and is basically a glass box enclosed within an elegant white skeletal frame. Foggo and Thomas's design, though not quite as radical as Farnsworth House, still reflects the same key principles.

Their house is a single-storey, flat-roofed structure with largely glass-clad walls enclosed within a black-painted, concrete frame. The architects strove to reduce extraneous detail to allow the simple shape and form of the building and the play of light in the interior to speak for themselves. The layout of the house consists of two wings, each with a lobby, two bedrooms and a bathroom, and a central core with a kitchen and a study on either side of the front entrance lobby. The open-plan entrance leads into a large reception room at the rear, opening onto landscaped gardens.

Light was a major consideration in the design – evident not only in the expanses of glass walls, but also through the insertion of roof lights, encouraging natural light into the very heart of the building. As the glazing is so predominant, the interior feels strongly connected with the outside – particularly when the wide patio doors are opened – and there are views across the gardens. Contrasting with the clear glass and adding textural interest are the rich, dark mahogany veneered panels that line most of the internal walls and the original beech flooring.

From the outside, the house has an almost translucent quality, and it is this, plus the fact that it is low-lying, which enables it to sit so unobtrusively within the surrounding landscape.

Opposite: *The low-lying building opens out onto landscaped gardens, and the connection with nature is enhanced by the use of beech flooring and dark mahogany veneered wall panels inside* (above).

The Fieldend development in Strawberry Hill, Twickenham, is one of the finest surviving housing estates built in the 1960s and has remained remarkably unaltered since its completion in 1961. It was one of many building projects undertaken in the post-war years to provide urgently needed new homes – in particular small family dwellings – for a burgeoning population. This was also a period when serious consideration was being given to improving social conditions and the projection of social ideologies. One of the numerous companies undertaking such building projects was Span Developments Ltd, founded in the late 1950s by architects Eric Lyons and Geoffrey Townsend, who frequently teamed up with landscape designer Ivor Cunningham and built around 2,000 homes in the United Kingdom during the height of their success in the 1960s, including the development at Fieldend.

The uniqueness of Span housing lies in the relationship between high-quality building and the overall layout and landscaping, designed hand in hand.

Given the housing crisis, the homes needed to be quick to construct and economical to build, while also providing excellent living conditions for families. They were intended to reflect the modern age, with Lyons greatly influenced by the designs of Walter Gropius (1883–1969), a leading Modernist architect in Germany and founder of the famous Bauhaus School.

Built on land left derelict after bombing in 1940, Fieldend consists of 51 houses, which are arranged in three public 'squares' set in several acres of landscaped gardens, specifically designed to foster community spirit. The landscaping was crucial to the overall plan, with open spaces considered one of the fundamentals of healthy living, particularly for those in built-up urban areas. The entire

development is geared towards creating a safe and idyllic environment for people of all ages. Winding paths wend their way through the grounds, encouraging residents to walk and to interact, and the parking facilities are located at some distance away from the houses – this was felt to be instrumental in encouraging people to mingle with one another. There are also carefully laid-out play areas for young children. The Residents Association manages the maintenance of the grounds and exterior of the buildings, as well as the social aspects of Fieldend.

All the houses are two storey and built of brick, with weatherboarding cladding, broad, two-tone, timber 'picture' windows (which frame outside views), a glazed front porch (with space for a pram) and a flat roof. Inside, the homes are light and

spacious, originally featuring an open-plan living room/study area, with attention to quality in both the design and the build. In addition to the extensive landscaping and open shared space, which comes up to the front door, each property also has a small, private rear garden.

As a mark of Fieldend's success, it was awarded a Housing Gold Award in 1961 and a Civic Trust Award in 1962, and in recognition of its architectural and social importance it was designated a Conservation Area by the London Borough of Richmond Upon Thames in 2005. But Fieldend's greatest validation is almost certainly the affection with which it is held by the residents, many of whom have never moved or have left and come back.

Opposite: *The safe environment of Fieldend has play areas for children and the outdoor spaces and winding paths encourage neighbours in the development to interact.*
Above: *Eric Lyons' careful attention to design gives bright, spacious interiors, which have influenced good design in the adaptation of rooms for contemporary living.*

COMMUNITY, LEARNING AND STUDIOS

'Just like we revel in the details of the architecture from previous pioneers and eras, we need to mark our own age within our architecture, so that future generations can enjoy the best that we could design.'

Open House London visitor

Perhaps more than any other major global city, London is made up of many communities and villages, which over time have merged to create the capital, while retaining their individual characters. At the heart of each community and neighbourhood are the public buildings that provide essential services, whether school, nursery, health centre, place of worship, library or other community resource. Alongside these buildings are also those facilities, such as studios, that provide support and resources to professionals, such as dance and theatre companies. While grand 'statement' architecture is of course vital for a capital city, it is often the less prominent, but well-designed local buildings that we pass by and enter regularly that have the greatest impact on our lives.

Community buildings inevitably reflect the underlying social and political attitudes of their times: the then avant-garde Arts and Crafts style of Mary Ward House, for example, mirrors the progressive philosophy behind the 'settlement' that it housed, expressly intended to bring together, and foster a spirit of community across, professional and working-class sectors of society in late Victorian London.

In more recent times, the community building, often purpose-built, has become a driver for regeneration, not only in the sense of providing a neighbourhood focus but also, on a practical level, as a convenient 'one-stop shop' housing a wide range of community facilities. This is particularly important in areas of economic and social disadvantage, where a new building can often become an important landmark and a revitalising force. Undoubtedly, buildings that are enjoyed by those who use them can inspire a sense of pride, which in turn has noticeably positive effects on the community as a whole.

Key to the success of such buildings are generally the inclusion of a central meeting area, and a careful consideration of layout and circulation that enables the visitor to navigate the spaces easily, along with varied textures, colours and well-lit spaces that provide a more welcoming environment than the traditional, closed nature of many institutional buildings. With continuous changes anticipated in service provision, these spaces are designed to be flexible to fulfil a great number of functions.

Today, good design is universally recognised as one of the factors in creating successful learning environments. With Building Schools for the Future and other recent educational policy agendas, school design has again become a focus for contemporary architects. Like health centres, schools have transformed into facilities for the whole community to use year-round, with the integration of, for example, sports centres and adult learning suites. The school building has itself also become an invaluable teaching tool, particularly in relation to sustainability, so that pupils and their teachers can begin to understand the real impact on their environment.

Lumen United Reformed Church, WC1

Lumen United Reformed Church offers a corner of tranquillity close to the heart of King's Cross. The original church on this site was a Gothic building, which suffered irreparable bomb damage during World War II and was consequently replaced with a new building, which opened in 1965. Very different in style from the original, the Regent Square Presbyterian Church (as it was then known) reflected the pared-down, modern architecture that is typical of the post-war era.

In 2007, the church commissioned architects Theis and Khan to redesign, update and extend the building because they wanted to make it more open to wider community use. It was renamed Lumen United Reformed Church. Three main elements constituted their design: an inspiring new 'sacred space'; a community café; and an extension that houses new community areas, which include two purpose-built, multifunctional rooms and a small art-gallery area. The central interior space is used for church services on Sundays, but is also flexible enough to be used as a further community space when necessary, for example for lectures or meetings.

Set within the main body of the church is the sacred space, known as the Shaft of Light – a striking, freestanding structure shaped like a giant, slanting, white-rendered cone, 11 metres (36 feet) high, with a single opening in the roof. The Shaft of Light offers a secluded area for worship or private gatherings. The enclosed 'room' feels protected and a world away from the busy London streets outside. The lack of decorative detailing encourages undistracted contemplation.

The exterior of the building is plain, simple and geometric in form, but the

Above: The façade of the building is enlivened by a vast window and bronze screen, which reveals the community café within.

façade is greatly enlivened by the new café, with its warm and welcoming interior that is clearly visible from the street and encourages visitors from all backgrounds to enter. Decorating the vast glass frontage is a bronze, three-dimensional, spiralling sculptural screen by contemporary artist Rona Smith, which evokes the traditional imagery of numerous faiths. Art and sculpture are also important in the interior. There is a small gallery to display work by artists and photographers, and the church features works by artist Alison Wilding, who has created a new font, a drinking fountain and a garden fountain.

To the rear of the church, a new courtyard garden has been created out of a former car park, and this now provides a peaceful open space. The newly formed community rooms are arranged around the garden and open out onto this area.

As a result of the outstanding transformation of this church the project won a RIBA Award in 2009.

Opposite:
Dominating the interior is the Shaft of Light, a freestanding 11-metre-high (36 feet) white cone, which provides a secluded area for worship or private gatherings.

Ismaili Centre, SW7

Located in South Kensington, facing the Victoria and Albert Museum, the Ismaili Centre occupies an important site on Cromwell Road. Inaugurated in 1985 by the then Prime Minister Margaret Thatcher, it was the first Ismaili Centre opened in the West and caters for the religious, social and cultural needs of London's sizeable Shia Imami Ismaili Muslim community. Another key aim of the centre is to encourage community integration through cultural exploration, and events are often held at the centre for members of the public from all religious and cultural backgrounds.

As the building is located on an 'island' site, there was a rare opportunity to design a building with presence, conceived in the round. The architects Casson Conder Partnership had to meet a range of criteria. On a practical level, the centre needed to provide a place for worship, religious education, community activities, committee meetings and events, as well as an art gallery. In addition, the new building had to be in the spirit of Islamic architecture while blending in with the eclectic mix of surrounding structures.

One of the few unifying elements between the various buildings in this area is the use of pale stone for façades, so the architects decided to use light-coloured materials, in keeping with the traditional Islamic architectural idiom. As a result, the exterior sits remarkably comfortably alongside the neighbouring façades, and the striking modern design with Islamic aesthetics – strong, regular shapes and simple lines – seems to be entirely appropriate in the setting.

The entrance hall, designed by German Muslim Karl Schlamminger, also adheres to the strong emblematic significance of lines and geometric forms that are so prevalent within the Islamic tradition. This is most clearly manifested in the patterned floor and reference to the number seven – a holy number in Islam, seen in the seven-sided pillars surrounding a seven-sided fountain.

However, the main focus of the Ismaili Centre is the enormous Prayer Hall, and the building is designed to guide the visitor towards this spiritual space. The hall's imminence is indicated in tiny details, such as slight changes in the patterns on the carpets, which escalate with proximity to the hall. The 'journey' to the Prayer Hall leads past a large Social Hall, with opulent light fittings and carpets designed by Schlamminger, and the Shoe Hall, where worshippers remove their shoes before entering the Prayer Hall. Schlamminger also designed the interior of this sacred space, which is entered through ornate, Islamic-style doors and lit by hundreds of tiny lamps.

On the roof of the building is an open-air garden, designed by the architects in association with Sasaki Associates and Lanning Roper as an integral part of the building, with an open courtyard on the top floor linking interior and exterior spaces. The combination of hard landscaping, planting and a series of fountains creates a tranquil space in the midst of this busy cultural quarter.

Opposite: *The building reflects the traditional Islamic architectural idiom while blending well with surrounding structures.*

Left: *Use of Islamic patterns also prevails within, seen here in the fountain and geometric floor design of the entrance hall.*

Below: *The landscaping of the rooftop open-air garden provides a tranquil space.*

The BAPS Shri Swaminarayan Mandir was the first traditional Hindu stone temple, or Mandir, to be built in Europe. It was designed by Indian temple architect C. B. Sompura, under the direction of guru Pramukh Swami Maharaj, the fifth spiritual successor of Bhagwan Swaminarayan (to whom the temple is dedicated), and was finished in 1995. The Mandir owes its existence largely to the local Hindu community, who raised funds and helped with the construction work on a voluntary basis.

An oasis of Hindu culture in Neasden, north-west London, the temple performs various functions, including providing a place for worship, learning, socialising, community events, celebrating festivals, music, art, sports and some healthcare services. It also houses a permanent exhibition, 'Understanding Hinduism', which helps non-Hindus to understand the concepts of Hindu culture and religion.

The enormous, two-storey white temple, complete with seven pinnacles and six domes, was built in accordance with the Hindu religion, which involves performing a number of rites during the course of construction. Over 2,800 tonnes of Bulgarian limestone were used for the exterior and 2,000 tonnes of Italian Carrara marble for the interior, which was shipped to India to be carved by more than 1,500 local craftsmen before being transported back to the United Kingdom. In all, 26,300 finished carved pieces were fitted together on site.

As is traditional for a sacred building, the temple is constructed so every piece of masonry is load-bearing to negate the need for any metal structural support. This accords with a belief that metals concentrate the earth's magnetic field and consequently impede meditation. The profusely carved, cantilevered central dome is believed to be the only one in Britain that does not use steel or lead.

The interior features elaborate decorative detail, with its marble staircase and many carved columns that depict deities and Hindu motifs. Beneath each of the pinnacles is a shrine housing sacred images of the deities within altars. Each aspect of the building's design and patterns is perfectly proportioned and believed to link the Mandir to the stars, planets and galaxies.

Next to the Mandir is the Haveli, a multifunctional cultural centre richly carved from wood in the traditional (Haveli) courtyard style of Gujarat.

Above: The carved columns inside the building feature Hindu deities and motifs.

Situated deep in the heart of the City of London, the historic Bevis Marks Synagogue – spiritual home to the Spanish and Portuguese (Sephardic) Jewish community – was completed in 1701 and is the oldest synagogue still in use in the United Kingdom. The architect Joseph Avis, who was a Quaker, won the commission for the synagogue in 1699. On completing the building, Avis refused to take payment, not wishing to profit from the construction of a place of worship.

The plain exterior of the synagogue reflects the architect's Quaker beliefs and was also inspired by non-conformist meeting rooms of the period. Modest and rectangular, it is constructed from red brick with Portland stone detailing and has two tiers of unadorned windows, those on the ground floor being smaller in size than those on the first floor. The roof, which was destroyed by fire in 1738 and repaired in 1749, is said to have incorporated a substantial oak beam that came from a Royal ship and was presented to the synagogue by Queen Anne (1665–1714).

Simple but effective design continues through the interior and reflects the influence of Sir Christopher Wren (see page 64), who was overseeing the rebuilding of the City's churches following the Great Fire in 1666, as well that of the Spanish and Portuguese Great Synagogue of Amsterdam, built in 1675. The interior has changed little since it was completed and still contains original furnishings as well as benches from the 1650s. It has a gallery (for women), supported on 12 Doric columns that symbolise the tribes of Israel, and a magnificent Renaissance-style Echal (ark), which contains the Torah scrolls and appears to be made from coloured Italian marble, but is actually painted oak. The Echal is flanked by ten candlesticks, which represent the Ten Commandments. The Corinthian columns reflect the style of altar pieces in a number of Wren churches.

Apart from the Echal, the most dominant features of the interior are seven hanging brass candelabra that represent the days of the week, with the largest (the Sabbath) hanging in the centre of the building. This was a gift to Bevis Marks from the community of the Great Synagogue in Amsterdam, and is lit, together with the other candelabra, for special occasions such as festivals and wedding ceremonies.

Above: Many of the original furnishings remain in the synagogue.

St Martin-in-the-Fields, WC2

This landmark Anglican church on the north-west corner of Trafalgar Square has, over the course of its long history, become a focal point for the local and wider community. During World War I, vicar Dick Sheppard offered the church as a refuge for soldiers on their way to war and coined it 'the church of the ever-open door'. This philosophy continues today, and it has become a stalwart supporter of the homeless, offering care through The Connection at St Martin's. Since the 1960s, it has held weekly services for the Chinese congregation and now houses a day centre to support Chinese people in need. The church also has an extensive underground space in the crypt, which is used for concerts, recitals and art exhibitions and houses a book and gift shop, a café and the London Brass Rubbing Centre.

The present church was designed by James Gibbs and finished in 1726, but documents indicate that there has been a church on this site since at least 1222. The design is based on that of a Roman temple, and has greatly influenced other church architecture, particularly in the United States. It has a distinctive portico and a pediment supported by massive Corinthian columns; steps lead from street level to the portico and are a popular meeting place. Above is a tall, elegant steeple with a gilt crown. The long sides of the building are seven bays in width, with the bays delineated by huge Corinthian pilasters.

The interior reflects the influence of Sir Christopher Wren (see page 64) and is similar to his church of St James's in Piccadilly, finished in 1684. The walls are pale and there is gold detailing throughout.

In 2006, Eric Parry Architects undertook an extensive programme of restoration and regeneration, injecting contemporary elements into this historic site. The brief was to create a masterplan that would unify the different elements of the site and create a series of uplifting spaces flexible in use. They added a freestanding new glass entrance pavilion, which leads to the foyer and the crypts, and a sunken glass lightwell brings daylight into the underground areas; the churchyard was also turned into a space for contemplation and socialising, while the underground spaces have been restored to provide improved visitor and community facilities. Conservation work to the church has removed Victorian additions, and clear handmade glass has replaced the translucent glazing, bringing light into the interior, with the installation of a new east window by leading contemporary artist Shirazeh Houshiary.

With its vibrant programme of events and cultural, religious and social ethics, St Martin-in-the-Fields is an important community and public hub as well as one of London's finest 18th-century buildings.

Above: *A sunken lightwell allows daylight into the underground parts of the building, and contemporary and historic elements of the site are unified.*

N ew Heart for Bow is the name assigned to the Victorian church of St Paul's, which was built in 1878 and closed in 1991 owing to the fact it was severely dilapidated and suffering from neglect. By the late 1990s, it was declared unsafe and had reached a point where it needed to be demolished or restored.

In 1998, it was decided that the church – once such an important part of this East End community – should be totally overhauled to create a multipurpose community centre to serve residents. Matthew Lloyd Architects (see also page 87) were commissioned by the Revd Philippa Boardman and the parochial church council to undertake the restoration, which was started in 2001 and finished in 2004. Funding for the project came from the New Opportunities Fund, the Heritage Lottery Fund, the Community Fund and local diocesan resources.

The design concept revolves around a 'building within a building', realised through the insertion of a giant, tulipwood-clad 'ark', or 'pod', raised on

curving steel columns inside the original church. This wooden structure provides two internal floors plus a mezzanine level. The ark, which is a striking modern element within the Victorian structure, has windows that provide views down into the interior of the old church and out across Bow. The unusual grain of the tulipwood gives the structure a distinctive character.

The top floor houses a gym and the first floor a flexible community space, currently used as a study support centre for children from disadvantaged backgrounds. On the ground floor there is a café, space for meditation and worship, a flexible meeting hall and several ancillary areas that serve a variety of functions.

This regeneration of an existing building has created a much-needed, thriving community centre at the heart of this area of east London, and it is an excellent example of contemporary architecture being used to inspire and change lives.

Above: The striking tulipwood-clad 'ark', set within the original church.

Mary Ward House, WC1

Mary Ward House, designed in 1895 by young architects Cecil Brewer and Dunbar Smith and built 1896–98, is one of London's finest complete examples of Arts and Crafts architecture. It was created specifically to house the 'Settlement' founded by pioneering social reformer Mary Ward (1851–1920), who was also a best-selling Victorian novelist known as Mrs Humphry Ward. Inspired by the leading intellectuals of the day, including designer William Morris, poet Alfred, Lord Tennyson and essayist/historian Thomas Carlyle, the aim was to bring education, culture, training and care to less privileged members of society. The driving philosophy behind the building was to break down class barriers and foster a unilateral community spirit by creating an environment in which the working classes and professionals could come together under one roof.

Originally called the Passmore Edwards Settlement after its benefactor the philanthropist John Passmore Edwards (1823–1911), the centre provided accommodation for young middle-class professionals, who could pass on their skills to local people in their leisure time, and social clubs were open to all to encourage cross-class socialising and learning. For a small annual membership fee, locals could attend interest groups in subjects as diverse as music, chess and debating, as well as gain practical advice from domestic-economy classes, self-help groups, retraining classes for the unemployed and a lawyer service for the poor. Music and lectures also formed an important part of the programme, with composer Gustav Holst acting as Music Director for a period and playwright George Bernard Shaw being among the luminary guest speakers. The building also housed the first school in England to have fully equipped classrooms for children with physical disabilities.

Brewer and Smith won a competition for the design and this was their first major project. The building was an articulate response to the inner-city housing crisis of the 19th century, and the design reflected the aims of the Settlement. Above the main entrance and on top of the porch are two stone eggs – the symbols of creation and perhaps suggesting the beginning of a new society born through social reform. The windows provide interest to the exterior and large, elegant dormer windows are set into the sloping slate roof. The back of the house faces onto a large, tranquil courtyard and gardens – a rare bonus for this busy area of London.

Inside, the house is effortlessly elegant, achieved through the proportions of the rooms with their high ceilings. The decorative scheme is simple with natural colouring, wood floors and touches of ornamental Arts and Crafts detail, for example in the stained glass set into some of the windows and the tiled fireplaces. Throughout, there is a balance between plain geometric lines and curvilinear, organic touches.

Following Ward's death, the house became a women's settlement before ceasing to be residential in 1961, when it was acquired by the National Institute for Social Work. It is now privately owned and used as a conference and exhibition centre, and has been sympathetically restored.

Opposite: *The building has a simple decorative scheme, with wood floors and touches of Arts and Crafts detailing.*

Left: *The building's brightly-coloured façade has intermittent glazing to reveal the interiors. The exposed concrete ceilings are a part of the building's environmentally sustainable features* (opposite).

The Coin Street Neighbourhood Centre forms the fourth side to the courtyard surrounded by the Iroko Housing Co-operative, and provides much-needed resources for the local and wider South Bank and Bankside communities. Haworth Tompkins Architects (see also page 180) designed both the housing and the community centre, completing the latter in 2007. It was financed mainly by Coin Street Community Builders with the support of various other organisations, such as the London Development Agency (now part of the Greater London Authority), the Waterloo Project Board, and Lambeth and Southwark councils. The neighbourhood centre forms one of the most recent parts of the Coin Street Community Builders' programme to transform a largely derelict site into a thriving mixed-use neighbourhood.

The centre provides a diverse range of affordable onsite facilities and services for local residents, including a crèche, youth groups, adult support programmes and leisure activities. In addition, it includes offices, conference rooms and meeting areas, as well as a café, restaurant and food shop. The aim of bringing people together and fostering a sense of community spirit is reflected in the design, and since opening the building has become a lively and important focus for families.

The most distinctive feature of the building is its vibrant, multicoloured street façade, which was the result of collaboration between the architects and Polish artist Antoni Malinowksi. It includes solar 'chimneys', to naturally ventilate the building using the sun's heat to draw air from the cooler north elevation overlooking Iroko Garden. Other sustainable features include solar panels for heating hot water, a system that harvests rainwater for flushing the lavatories, interior lights operated via sensors and a stringent system of recycling waste within the building. The careful balance of glazed and non-glazed areas allows natural light to enter the building while keeping heat gain from the sun to a minimum.

Outdoor areas provide secure, partially enclosed spaces for the community to use and enjoy, most notably the central gardens, which lie at the heart of the complex, and the landscaped terraces including the roof terrace, with spectacular views. The outdoor spaces and timber panelling act as a visual link between the community centre and the three surrounding blocks of housing, creating a sense of unity within the complex.

Part of the success of this building is its flexibility and the fact it can be adapted easily for any number of uses in response to changing demands.

These studios, designed by Sarah Wigglesworth Architects and opened in 2006, were commissioned by the choreographer Siobhan Davies CBE to provide a permanent home for her dance company founded in 1988, which had until then lived a peripatetic existence. In addition, the building provides rehearsal facilities for other dance companies, classes for the local community and has a rolling visual arts programme.

The project involved the refurbishment and extension of a redundant, three-storey, late-Victorian school building located in the playground of a primary school in

Southwark, south-east London. The new development houses two dance studios, changing and therapy rooms, a large foyer, offices and meeting rooms.

Undoubtedly, the highlight is the main dance studio. One of Wigglesworth's aims for the design was to create a place where both the performers and the architecture

Opposite: *The sail-like arches of the ceiling of the main dance studio are clearly visible from the exterior* (above). *Stairs suspended from steel rods* (left) *rise from the foyer, and allow light in and offer a view outwards.*

would appear to 'dance together in the sky', so she created a new studio on top of the old building, beneath a distinctive roof that comprises a series of large, sculptural, blue-grey 'shells'. Inside, the studio has a spacious, minimalist feel. Below the 5-metre (16-foot) high ceiling, a series of smooth, undulating birch-ply arches seem to swell and float weightlessly above the dancers, and the room is filled with daylight that filters through roof lights set into the arches. The light is controlled to ensure it is always ambient, never becoming too bright or distracting by casting dramatic shadows, and there are no mirrors or bars on the walls – just a simple, sprung timber floor covered in linoleum. This is an uplifting space ideal for creative work, calm and concentration. Unlike the second, smaller studio, it can also be used as a performance venue, accommodating an audience of up to 100 people.

The central foyer has high walls that stretch upwards to the underside of the rooftop studio. A lime green column rises through the space, tilted at an angle as if in a dance pose, and adds to the sense of creativity and dynamism that is apparent throughout the building. The stairs, which are suspended from steel rods, rise from the back of the foyer and offer views out; they also make a criss-cross pattern on the rear-facing glass façade, cleverly breaking up views into the building. Halfway up the stairs and overlooking the entrance is a balcony lined in red leather – it is a place where dancers can meet, stretch, rest and see what is happening, both outside and inside the building.

Wigglesworth's joining of old and new in the Siobhan Davies Studios has resulted in an exhilarating new space. The project is a prime example of how to bring new use to existing buildings in a sustainable and innovative way. The building is fully accessible to those with disabilities and includes many sustainable materials and features. Winner of a RIBA Award, 2006, it is a triumph of collaboration between the client and architect.

Jerwood Space, SE1

Jerwood Space is a major project undertaken by the charitable Jerwood Foundation, which supports the arts, culture and education. It provides much-needed, affordable rehearsal space for theatre and dance companies (with an emphasis on young, emerging professional groups), as well as a café, a public art gallery and a glass-covered courtyard.

The building occupies the site of the former Orange Street School, constructed in 1872 and designed by architect E. R. Robson of the London School Board; over the course of 100 years or so, it was used for various other educational institutions. The structure suffered substantial damage in World War II, which destroyed the top floors, and was in a state of some disrepair when it was acquired by the Jerwood Foundation in 1997.

Paxton Locher Architects were commissioned to transform the Victorian building into a bright, clean theatre and dance rehearsal space, and it is now the largest such space in London.

The architects made as much use as possible of the existing building, allowing its character and history to show through. They completely reused the existing outer shell and retained some internal elements such as glazed brickwork and several fittings. Five new rehearsal spaces were created, with the two main spaces on each of the ground and first floors being connected by doors that can be opened to provide a single substantial floor space.

Natural light has always played an important part in the building's appeal: the original architect, Robson, included large windows to introduce maximum light into the classrooms; Paxton Locher inserted opaque glass walls separating the male and female showers and covered the art gallery and café, which were converted from three former outbuildings (used variously in the past as a wash-house, car inspection pit and bike sheds) in glass. The new roof of the main gallery reused the original metal roof trusses exposed. In 2005, Satellite Architects created The Glasshouse, adding a steel-and-glass structure in the existing courtyard to extend the café and gallery area.

In 2006, Munkenbeck and Partners were commissioned to add a roof extension to replace the upper floors that had been destroyed during the War. The contemporary extension, which was designed to appear lighter than the rest of the building, and to have its own definitive character nevertheless complements the existing structure and the surrounding area. The architects used materials such as Corten steel (which weathers), stainless steel and timber louvres, and set the cladding back from the face of the existing building to prevent rust staining the brickwork. The upper floor is a totally glazed box that during daytime blends with the sky, and at night, when illuminated, radiates an unearthly glow.

Throughout the building the interiors are simple and unconstrained, making them inspirational places for a wide variety of creative endeavours.

Opposite: *The site of a former Orange Street School has been transformed into the largest theatre and dance rehearsal space in London.*
Above: *Space 7, the largest studio in Jerwood Space.*
Left: *Visitors listen to a performance taking place in The Glasshouse.*

Waldron Health Centre, SE14

One of the largest healthcare facilities of its kind in Britain, the Waldron Health Centre in Lewisham, south-east London, was completely redeveloped on its original site by architects Henley Halebrown Rorrison (formerly Buschow Henley) and opened in 2008. The Waldron was designed with the whole community in mind, not just visitors to the health centre, and aims to embody a 'joined up' approach to the delivery of primary healthcare, with services including dentistry and ante-/post-natal care as well as GP surgeries.

Situated on a busy main road by New Cross station, and framing a new civic square, the 100-metre (328-foot) long Waldron building creates a new focus for the area's urban landscape. High metallic lettering spells out the centre's name, and the lacquered, cherry-coloured, timber-clad façade creates an attractive and

welcoming front. The development also contains several retail units, with further shops and apartments planned.

The design was based on a Z-shaped layout, and the architects carefully considered the movement of people around the building. Patients enter from the public square into the spacious, five-storey-high, top-lit atrium, which features a winding wooden staircase and a specially designed installation by Martin Richman. From here, landings on each floor lead to four independently run surgeries, each with its own waiting room and treatment

Suite 5 • Amersham Vale Training Practice

Suite 4

1

rooms. Placing the treatment rooms at the end of the circulation system ensures that the flow of 'traffic' is reduced and the patients' and doctors' privacy maintained. Although each clinic has an identical internal arrangement, each feels different because of its position within the building. Floor-to-ceiling windows allow plenty of light into the building, and every corridor, waiting room and treatment room has a view to the outside. The whole building is elevated slightly on a plinth, to ensure people outside cannot look into the treatment rooms.

The natural feel created by the wood façade is enhanced by two courtyard gardens. However, the urban quality of the surrounding area is retained in the building's bold design.

The colours of the interior are still warm, but less imposing in beige and greys to create a sense of calm. Wooden louvres on the east and west sides act as sunshades and acoustic baffles, muting the noise from outside.

The Waldron Health Centre's striking design has made it a local landmark, and a vital part of the area's regeneration.

Opposite: *The bold cherry-coloured timber-clad façade hides a spacious top-lit atrium with a winding wooden staircase* (above).

Health Centres {151}

Left: *The exterior of the building has a distinctive cantilevered form, while bright art works and signs inside the Health Centre make it feel more like an arts space* (opposite).

Completed in 2008, the new Kentish Town Health Centre, designed by architects Allford Hall Monaghan Morris (see also pages 14, 104, 160) in collaboration with local design champion Dr Roy Macgregor and Camden and Islington Community Solutions, sets a definitive new standard for the National Health Service. The building houses a large GP practice, a dentist, paediatric and children's services, screening programmes, a library and a number of offices and meeting rooms for staff. The building is the result of a design competition initiated by Dr Macgregor to create a centre that expresses and incorporates the new holistic approach to healthcare.

The site itself presented some problems, because it was small and bordered to one side by protected trees. To compensate for this restricted space at ground-floor level, the architects designed this new, three-storey-high building with a small ground-floor plan that then cantilevers out on the upper floors. This allows for car parking beneath the projecting elements on one side, while on the other the building sits in close proximity to the trees. The design concept has been described by the architects as resembling the game Jenga, and indeed in appearance this is what the building looks like – the different health departments have been pieced together and then pulled out or pushed in, like the pieces of the children's game, resulting in an irregular, boxy exterior. The building responds to the form, scale and materials of the surrounding housing.

The façade has been treated simply, with a white render and repetitive square windows, some of which have distinctive lime-green metal panels punctured with a series of small openings to allow air through when the windows are opened on the inside. The interiors are similarly plain, with a base palette of white, but are then greatly enhanced by bold, brightly coloured art works and signs created by graphic designers Studio Myerscough. The whole of the interior feels like an art gallery or a performing arts space, and is notably light.

A central 'street' runs through the middle of the building, bringing together the various services and making it easy for visitors to find their way around. Public and clinical space occupies the ground and first floors, while staff space and teaching rooms are on the second floor. The waiting-room area on the ground floor has views up through the building to the floors (and activity) above, providing interest and diversion in a place that can be associated with worry and ill health.

This inspiring building was shortlisted for the RIBA Stirling Prize in 2009.

Maggie's Centres provide emotional and practical support for anyone affected by cancer and their families, carers and friends. The idea for these centres was conceived by cancer patient Maggie Keswick Jencks. Her vision was to create places where people with cancer could access and share information about the disease, find out about medical treatments and learn from other sufferers in a welcoming, domestic environment. Working with Maggie to develop her ideas were her husband, architect and writer Charles Jencks, and her oncology nurse, Laura Lee. Maggie died in 1995, and one year later the first Maggie's Centre was opened in Edinburgh. Today, Maggie's Centres are found across England and Scotland, with ongoing plans for new centres in Wales, Hong Kong, Barcelona and additional ones in England.

All Maggie's Centres are purpose-built with several design principles at their core – they have to be sufficiently large to cope with many people, yet still feel personal, friendly and comfortable rather than institutional, and need to be easy to navigate and make the visitor feel protected and secure. Gardens are also an important aspect of the cancer-care Centres, as both Maggie and Charles shared a passion for landscape architecture.

These design principles are all fundamental to the West London Maggie's Centre, which was designed by Rogers Stirk Harbour and Partners (see also pages 18, 22, 40, 162) and constructed between 2001 and 2008. It was the first purpose-built cancer centre in England and won the 2009 RIBA Stirling Prize. At one-and-a-half storeys high, the building is domestic in scale and feels more like a home than a public building. It is attached to the London Charing Cross Hospital in Hammersmith,

and to overcome the noisy, frenetic nature of the site on the busy Fulham Palace Road, the architects designed an insular building with protective, closed-off walls that shield the rooms inside. Fast-growing birch trees were planted along the two walls that face the busy main road and the hospital to further shelter the building and absorb some of the noise.

The entrance to the centre is within the hospital grounds, and specially designed gardens by landscape designer Dan Pearson lead towards the front door, which is reached via a winding path that guides past flower beds, stone sculptures and wooden benches. The visitor is immediately struck by the vibrant, brilliant red-orange colour of the external walls and the metal roof, which appears to 'float' above the building; the colour is instantly positive.

The interior layout is also similar to that of a house. At its heart is an open-plan kitchen/living room with a double-height ceiling, and all the internal space radiates from this one communal area. On the ground floor there are three sitting rooms, a library, a number of smaller, private spaces for personal conversations and internal courtyard gardens, also designed by Pearson, with light flooding through the glass roof and walls into the interior. Further increasing the sense of homeliness and relaxing atmosphere is the inclusion of three fireplaces in the design, which make natural meeting points for visitors, and comfortable designer furnishings. Upstairs, the space is arranged into a number of smaller, more intimate rooms, which provide greater privacy. However, they are all glazed from waist height upwards, so the sense of transparency and communication throughout the building is maintained. An open mezzanine level contains office space and terraces so that

staff can work but still continue to interact with visitors.

The whole building is designed to be relatively flexible, allowing for a variety of activities to be held there, from lunch clubs to yoga classes, as well as informal socialising, meetings, reading and simply escaping the world at large for a short period. An important element of the centre's design was to make people feel at home and have a sense of ownership of the space rather than simply feeling like a visitor, and in this way could be encouraged to return to the centre as frequently as they desired.

In 2008, Maggie's Centre West London was opened by Sarah Brown (Maggie's patron and wife of the then Prime Minister Gordon Brown) and writer and presenter Nigella Lawson (whose first husband, journalist John Diamond, had died of cancer a few years earlier). The centre has since provided vital support to thousands of visitors and their families.

Above: *A vibrant red-orange colour defines the external walls, along with its 'floating' metal roof. Overleaf: A double-height kitchen/living room sits at the heart of Maggie's Centre, and light floods in through the building's extensive glazing.*

Hammersmith Group Practice, W6

The Hammersmith Bridge Road Surgery, opened in 2001, has become a landmark piece of architecture within this busy area of west London. It is not a building that announces its function; in fact, with its unusual sculptural form it appears as if it could serve any number of purposes, from a place of worship to a contemporary art gallery or even an office. This is no coincidence – architect Guy Greenfield set out to design a building that would make a strong statement yet could accommodate a change of use if necessary in the future.

Greenfield's inspired design was his creative response to an extremely difficult curved site, which also had the disadvantage of being adjacent to the busy A4 flyover and Hammersmith roundabout. His solution was to create a curved floor plan and a heavily protective structure with an internal layout that would minimise noise levels inside the building.

The main façade consists of a monumental white wall comprising huge, curved panels forming a 'shield', interspersed with narrow strips of glass, to allow daylight into the interior. Although the wall looks like concrete, it is in fact made from lightweight metal frames covered in render and painted white – a less expensive and more eco-friendly option. The rear of the building is entirely covered in glass and looks onto a tranquil landscaped courtyard, while the roof and two end walls are clad in copper, which gives a warm resonance to the building and complements the simplicity of the other materials.

Inside, the plan is simple and easy for patients to navigate – a single internal corridor leads from the waiting area to the consulting rooms, which overlook the secluded courtyard. The floors are sea-green Cumbrian slate, which contrast with the white walls and turquoise and orange accents in the interior, and recall the aesthetics of the French giant of Modernism, Le Corbusier (1887–1965).

Shortlisted for the RIBA Stirling Prize 2001, this healthcare building has an energising interior and an extremely dramatic exterior – particularly at night, when the white walls are floodlit and take on an almost Mediterranean feel.

The Mediterranean aesthetic of this building (left) *extends from its white curve-panelled façade through to the sea-green floors, white walls and turquoise and orange accents of the interior* (above).

King's Cross Construction Skills Centre, N1

This large industrial building, designed by David Morley Architects and opened in March 2009, houses the flagship Construction Skills Centre, which forms part of the King's Cross regeneration programme – one of Europe's largest urban regeneration projects. Until the 18th and 19th centuries, this area of London was semi-rural, but with the arrival of the canals and then railways, it became an important transport and industrial hub. During the 19th century, this was one of the poorest areas of London and home to numerous slums.

Today, the site is undergoing a major transformation into a lively mixed-use area to include retail units, offices, a hotel, an open public square, the new Central Saint Martins (see pages 168–69), the restored Regent's Canal, a sports centre, library and various other uses, including the Construction Skills Centre – one of the first elements of this large project to be completed. The centre offers local people training opportunities within the construction industry, with the added incentive of leading to professional qualifications and employment opportunities on site. Carpentry, joinery, brick-laying and civil engineering make up the majority of the courses.

The Construction Skills Centre has a distinctive triangular plan, determined by the administrative boundary of the London Borough of Camden in which the building is located. It contains two storeys of support accommodation along York Way to the west, with a double-height workshop and classrooms on the upper level to the east. The classrooms have a strong visual connection to the workshop, reinforcing the link between academic study and practical application of skills. Crucially, the building's structure and detailing are

deliberately left 'unfinished', so students can learn from the construction. The underside of the ceiling and areas of wall are exposed, the plant room is caged rather than walled in the conventional sense, and the workshop floors and stairs are made from exposed concrete.

Roof lights run the length of the building, bringing natural light into the double-height workshop space below and creating a distinctive 'wave' profile that creates a dramatic look. With sustainability in mind, the green roof also features photovoltaic panels, to capture energy to run the electric lights and appliances.

As a mark of its success, the Construction Skills Centre won a RIBA Award in 2009 and has achieved a National Skills Academy Status. It has also provided an employment boost to the local community.

Above: Roof lights run the length of the building, bringing daylight into the workshop space and creating a distinctive profile to the building.

Westminster Academy, W2

The multi-award-winning Westminster Academy, which opened in 2006, represents a new departure for school buildings. It was designed by Allford Hall Monaghan Morris (see also pages 14, 104, 152) with considerable input from the Academy team, in particular the then Principal, Alison Banks.

Unlike traditional school buildings, Westminster Academy (which is sponsored by the Dangoor family through their Exilarch's Foundation) feels like a business or conference centre – appropriate for the academy's specialism, international business and enterprise. Designed to be inspirational for the students, it is a bright, bold diversion from its rather colourless, built-up location in west London, adjacent to the Westway flyover and surrounded by 1960s tower blocks.

Inspired by geological stratification, the main building – a five-storey rectangular block – has a striking façade consisting of large, horizontal bands of glazing and brilliantly coloured terracotta tiles, which are dark green on the lowest level and become progressively lighter until the yellow top tier, and a series of illuminated screens. These layers are reflective and vibrant during the day and glow like a beacon at night. The sports centre, which is clad mainly in timber with the end walls made entirely of glass, is housed in a separate block to allow for year-round community use. Both the main block and the sports facility have green roofs.

The hub of the building is the four-storey, glass-covered atrium, conceived as a vibrant, busy 'marketplace'. Classrooms lead from this impressive central space and have direct views onto it through their glass walls. It acts as an important social area and is also used for extra-curricular activities, community events and workshops. The scheme in the atrium uses colours that match the exterior façade and involves oversized and integrated graphics and words that highlight the Academy's core values – 'Global Citizenship', 'Communication' and 'Enterprise'. Also, suspended below the glazed roof is a series of brightly coloured panels, which shade the interior from the sun.

Teaching areas on the upper floors are as multifunctional as possible, responding to an integrated curriculum based not on subject areas but on generic themes and topics. Also reflecting the academy's specialism, 'breakout spaces', seminar rooms and lecture theatres are integrated into the design. Staff offices are on the top floor with access to a large roof terrace, while on the floors below deep-set balconies at the rear provide students with places to relax and socialise.

The success of this building, which was shortlisted for the RIBA Stirling Prize, 2008, and the driving forces behind it have been translated into the outstanding achievements of the pupils; in 2011, it was named in the top 40 of the 200 most-improved schools in England.

Built on the site of the former Hackney Downs School, in east London, the RIBA-Award-winning Mossbourne Community Academy was designed by Richard Rogers Partnership (now Rogers Stirk Harbour and Partners, see also pages 18, 22, 40, 154) and completed in 2004. In 2010, a new building was added by Studio E Architects (see also page 164) to accommodate the sixth form. The Academy is publicly funded with sponsorship by local, Hackney-born businessman, Sir Clive Bourne (son of Moss Bourne, after whom the Academy is named).

The core objectives of the Academy are to raise the aspirations, expectations and achievements of the students, with an uplifting building playing a key role in creating a positive learning environment. It was also designed as an engine of regeneration, with the wider community encouraged to use the learning facilities out of school hours.

The design of the Academy had to take account of the awkward site, which is a triangular plot bounded on two sides by a railway line and the third aspect overlooking parkland (Hackney Downs). To compensate for the noise of the railway, the architects designed a V-shaped building, with blank walls facing the railway tracks and the main focus of the school being concentrated inwards, around a large central courtyard.

The three-storey building is one of the largest timber-framed structures in the United Kingdom and has flexible teaching spaces to respond to changing needs. It is divided into sections, or terraced 'houses', which are accessed via a deeply recessed, covered cloister that acts like a street. Each 'house' contains a different faculty and features an open communal space, staff areas and IT resources on the ground floor and classrooms on the upper two storeys. Some of the internal partition walls can be easily removed or reconfigured with minimum disturbance to the rest of the school. From the classrooms, the students have views across the courtyard to the green, open parkland beyond – unusual in an inner-city school.

Under the helm of Founding Principal Sir Michael Wilshaw – who received a knighthood for services to education and was appointed HM Chief Inspector of Schools in England and Head of Ofsted in 2012 – Mossbourne Community Academy developed into one of the country's leading academies, with 86 per cent A* to C grades in its first GCSE results in 2009.

Left: *The Academy is divided into terraced 'houses', each containing a separate faculty. It is one of the largest timber-framed structures in the United Kingdom* (opposite).

Larmenier & Sacred Heart Catholic Primary School, W6

The Larmenier and Sacred Heart Catholic Primary School, which opened in 2007, was built to amalgamate the previously separate infant and junior schools, bringing them together under one roof. The contemporary design, by Studio E Architects (see also page 162), provides for the educational needs of the school while promoting the sustainable nature of the development, so that the pupils learn about the environment.

Staff, parents, community members and the 450 pupils themselves engaged with the design process, and were encouraged to participate actively in the creation of the school, nurturing a sense of achievement and pride in the finished building. This extended to a series of talks by specialists involved in the project to explain the ecological aspects to the children, enabling them to more fully understand the concepts behind the construction of their school. In addition, pupils were invited to visit the site at various stages of construction, so they could see for themselves how different elements fitted together and experience the school taking shape.

Two large plane trees dominated the chosen site for the new school and were retained, becoming the focus of the design and configuration. The shape of the two-storey, spiral building, centred on a courtyard, is determined by the mathematics of nature: the Fibonacci 'golden mean' defines the main circulation route. All the classrooms face onto the two trees and have direct access to external 'learning spaces', where children are encouraged to engage in practical, activity-based learning outside.

Sustainability was a prime consideration, with environmentally friendly features including a green roof, photovoltaic panels to capture energy for heating and hot water, and internal lightwells and roof lights to maximise levels of natural light and ventilation. In addition, timber from renewable resources was used for the roof, cladding, door frames and floors.

The pupils were set the task of designing their own graphic motif, to appear on the sunshade awnings and other areas of the building, such as the lightwells. Helped by an artist, the children devised a leaf motif, which ties in with the indoor–outdoor feel of the school and is fundamental to the building's green ethos.

Left: *The school building is centred around a courtyard, and throughout the building emphasis is placed on access to the outdoors, with the use of timber within, and roof lights maximising natural light* (opposite).

The Blizard Building – adjacent to the Royal London Hospital in Whitechapel, east London – houses the Blizard Institute of Cell and Molecular Science and is the largest institute of Barts and the London School of Medicine and Dentistry. Designed by Alsop Architects/ Amec and opened in 2005, it is named after Sir William Blizard (1743–1835), distinguished surgeon and one of the founders of the London Hospital Medical College. Bold and colourful, this building has actively rejected the traditional, sanitised environment of the laboratory and represents a real departure for research-institute design.

The main principles behind the design were to break down barriers between different scientific disciplines by bringing scientists together to work in the same space, and in so doing encourage the cross-fertilisation of ideas as well as interaction between colleagues. The aim was also to create an atmosphere of transparency and to highlight the building's function in as obvious a way as possible, creating a significant local landmark and resource for the community. Further considerations were to provide an educational resource for the local community and public exhibition space, and to create a building that was representative of a new 'face' for science – one that would be interesting and lively and dispel often common perceptions of science being dull.

The Institute consists of two architecturally distinct buildings on either side of an open 'mews', joined via a multicoloured glass bridge at first-floor level. The larger structure is a prominent, three-storey glass pavilion, which reveals the activity going on inside the building. The façade features decorative, opaque coloured panels by Scottish artist Bruce McLean, based on images taken from molecular science. Opposite this structure is a narrow, rectangular building called the Wall of Plant, so named because it houses the mechanical and electrical services needed for the complex laboratory work. A special zinc cladding system enables moving images and pictures to be projected onto the façade of this building from the roof of the pavilion opposite.

Stretching the full length of the site, set slightly below street level, is an expansive research floor, or laboratory. This research floor has the capacity for 400 scientists to work side by side in an open-plan environment, and is the largest such space

Left: *The multi-coloured glass bridge unites both elements of the Blizard Institute.* Opposite: *Four organically shaped 'pods' distinguish the pavilion, including the 'Cloud' and 'Spikey' and 'Mushroom' pods visible here.*

in the United Kingdom. Roof lights ensure the area receives plenty of natural light.

Visitors enter the building at the Wall of Plant and then cross the glass bridge to reach the pavilion. Once inside, they have a view of four, organically shaped 'pods', which are suspended above the open laboratory floor. The 'Mushroom' pod, which is open-topped and linked to the glass bridge, forms the entrance to the glass pavilion; a spiral staircase leads down directly into the laboratory below. The 'Centre of the Cell', which resembles a giant orange molecule and is the largest pod, provides two levels of floor space for an interactive learning display. The remaining two, smaller pods – the white, elliptical 'Cloud' and black, pointed, star-like 'Spikey' – are located at the opposite end of the pavilion and provide flexible meeting and seminar spaces. The galleries around the atrium are used by doctoral students and researchers for writing up experiments.

Bright colours are used unreservedly throughout the building, from the pinks, reds and purples of the joining glass bridge and the splashes of colour on the façade, to the strident orange walls of the main entrance, the brilliant red of the carpet in the glass pavilion and the dark green lecture theatre with contrasting fuchsia-coloured seats. The effect has generated great interest from both those working within the building and passers-by.

Reflecting its appeal, the Blizard Building has won a number of architectural awards, including a RIBA Award, 2006.

Central Saint Martins, N1

For many years, Central Saint Martins – part of the University of the Arts London and a college with a worldwide reputation for producing stellar creative talents in the areas of art, design and performance – was housed in five separate buildings in the West End. However, at the end of 2011, the college was able to move all its faculties into one impressive, newly developed building in King's Cross.

Stanton Williams Architects won the commission for the campus with their design that incorporates a 19th-century granary and two former transit sheds with two new, four-storey blocks at the centre of the King's Cross regeneration project. This development site, consisting of 67 acres of derelict land, has had a rich industrial and transport history and, once completed, will provide an exciting mixed-use area of business, retail, residential, creative and public space. The college faces onto London's newest public square (Granary Square) and the restored Regent's Canal.

The centrepiece of the new Central Saint Martin's is the old Granary, built in 1851 at the height of the railway boom. It was used for the storage and transportation of grain throughout eastern England and still retains many of its original Victorian features. An internal 'street', covered with a translucent roof that introduces natural light to the interior, runs the length of the site, acting as a central pathway and meeting place, with suspended walkways above and social areas, such as the café, leading from it. On-campus facilities include multipurpose workshops and specialist studios, a state-of-the-art lecture theatre, a library, gallery and research unit, a Performance Centre with public theatre, dance studios and rehearsal spaces, and an open-air terrace with spectacular views across London.

The campus is vast, providing around 10 acres of floor space, but nonetheless it retains cohesiveness throughout the different areas. The architects wanted the new space to meld seamlessly with the old and retain the strongly industrial feel of the original site. Consequently, they created robust spaces within the new buildings using industrial materials such as concrete and timber blocks. Also, they updated elements in the old building for contemporary use – for instance, by converting the old horse stables into student bike sheds, or installing the new lifts in the north wing of the Granary, where the original elevator system once transported grain to the silos.

The interior is markedly simple, which emphasises the building's stark beauty. With the long-term future in mind, the spaces are all designed to be as flexible as possible, and fairly neutral at the outset to allow each different artistic department to imprint their own character and identity on their particular areas.

The new Central Saint Martins is a state-of-the-art facility that not only fulfils the college's diverse needs but hopes to inspire creativity, communication and collaboration between students from a wide range of artistic disciplines.

Opposite (above and below): *The Granary is the centrepiece of the new Central Saint Martins building, featuring an internal 'street'.* Right: *A state-of-the-art facility needs an equally state-of-the-art façade.*

Opened in 2010, the Lightwell at the Royal Veterinary College is the newest addition to this historic centre of learning, transforming an under-used lightwell to create flexible spaces to augment the surrounding library, refectory, museum and teaching spaces. Established in 1791, the college has continued to grow exponentially since its beginnings, becoming a part of London University in 1949 and now having two campuses – the original one in Camden (with current buildings dating to 1935) and a large estate in Hertfordshire.

The Lightwell is a bright, vibrant courtyard at the heart of the Camden-based campus, on a tight site with limited room for expansion. At three storeys high, it is a key thoroughfare for the building, with the various functional aspects of the college, such as teaching rooms, library, museum, refectory, lecture hall and laboratories, reached via this exciting space, or looking down onto it. The college describes the Lightwell as its 'social learning project' – it is a place where students can study and socialise, and has been designed to provide both open, informal spaces and more intimate, closed spaces for when more intense concentration is required.

Architecture PLB was responsible for this conversion, and transformed the outdoor area by covering it with a transparent polymer (ETFE) roof. This material, which was perhaps more famously used for the biomes at the Eden Project, Cornwall, lets more light into the building than glass and is considerably lighter in weight and less expensive to install.

At ground level there is a café as well as seating areas, above which a 'pod', an extension to the library, 'hovers' in the space on tall, stilt-like legs. Made of pale plywood, the pod (which is another

area for learning and relaxing) has high enclosing walls with punched-out holes allowing views down to the café and seating areas below. On the staircase leading up to the pod there is a mezzanine where informal tutorials sometimes take place. The modern lines of the library pod and the café furniture and furnishings, complete with brightly coloured tables, contrast with the backdrop of the existing building's red-brick walls to create an overall contemporary feel.

Dotted around the brightly lit area, the skeletons of a two-year-old African elephant, a polar bear and a sloth climbing up a branch, as well as the skulls of a hippopotamus, gazelle and alligator, mingle with the students and staff, adding a humorous touch and leaving little doubt to the college's affiliations.

Opposite: *The wooden library 'pod' sits on stilt-like legs, and with its punched-out holes, provides* *a bright space for studying and relaxing above the café space below* (above).

A lesser building might have easily fallen in the shadow of such a formidable neighbour as the British Museum, but the sophisticated design of Senate House, with its distinctive geometric Portland stone façade, holds its own on the Bloomsbury skyline. Indeed, at the time of its construction (1932–37), Senate House was the tallest secular building in London, standing at 209 feet (64 metres).

Architect Charles Holden was appointed in 1931 – following his work on 55 Broadway (see page 28) and various London Underground stations – to design a permanent site for the University of London, which was then the largest university in the world. Holden originally intended a complex for the University, but due to a lack of funds these plans were never realised.

Holden carefully adhered to the brief of Vice-Chancellor William Beveridge to construct a building that 'could not have been built by any earlier generation than this': not only was Senate House's appearance strikingly modern, it was the first substantial building in the capital to employ electric heating, with use of an early storage heater – and an early form of air conditioning was also implemented.

Owing to a five-year multi-million-pound refurbishment to preserve and enhance original features, the building's main rooms can still be used for functions today. Holden himself took special care to design every detail of Beveridge Hall, in

order to make it the ideal space to gather for various purposes – and its continued use as such reflects his success. On the first floor, The Chancellor's Hall, with its grand Travertine marble, allows a more sunlit conference room, with four floor-to-ceiling windows on both its east and west sides. Perhaps most eye-catching of all is Crush Hall, which was constructed as a ceremonial space, as is evidenced by the marble and gold leaf décor. While now

more commonly used for conferences, it has seen its fair share of world leaders, including Winston Churchill. As well as the popularity of its halls for funcions, Senate House continues to house the University of London's library, and with updated office space and improved literary resources it is perfectly equipped to move the university into the future.

Senate House was the final design by Charles Holden ever to be constructed.

Its detractors claimed echoes of Nazi aesthetics, an accusation not helped by the rumour – false – that it was spared during the London bombings due to Hitler desiring it as a British headquarters for the Nazis. Its imposing nature was also supposed to have inspired George Orwell's 'Ministry of Truth' in his novel Nineteen Eighty-Four. However, the building has seen off its critics to become a much-admired example of 20th-century architecture.

Opposite: *The bold geometric façade of what was once the tallest secular building in London.* Above: *The Crush Hall, a striking ceremonial space within Senate House.*

Dulwich College traces its history to 1619, when it was founded by the famed Elizabethan actor Edward Alleyn, who purchased the estate of Dulwich and turned it into a school, with the initial purpose of educating '12 poor scholars'. Originally called Alleyn's College of God's Gift, the school was run according to Alleyn's principles that the pupils must have a rounded education, including the arts and good manners, and that it should be open to pupils from all social backgrounds.

As a result of its success and rapid expansion, the school moved to a new 70-acre grassland site on Dulwich Common in the 19th century. At the heart of this campus is the New College – a magnificent building designed by Victorian architect Charles Barry junior, eldest son of prominent architect Sir Charles Barry (see pages 205, 206). Barry was given free rein in his design and produced what he described as a building styled on 13th-century North Italian lines. The structure is essentially Palladian, but with the addition of eclectic and Gothic details, such as the triangular gables and ornate roof finials, turrets and cupolas, reminiscent of Barry's father's famous redesign of the Houses of Parliament. The building is expressly grand in its dimensions – to reflect the school's prestigious status and increasing number of pupils. The grandness continues to the interior, particularly the Great Hall and staircases; in addition, the school had three science laboratories and a lecture theatre, making it a market leader in its day in terms of facilities.

At the time it was built, New College was received with enthusiasm, and at the opening ceremony in 1870 the College Governors described it as 'worthy of our aspirations and resources'. Barry was

awarded a RIBA Gold Medal in 1877 in recognition of his service to architecture, with Dulwich College generally being considered his finest work. The medal was well deserved, despite the fact that Barry himself was President of RIBA the year it was awarded.

Throughout the 20th century, Dulwich College continued to expand, and additional buildings were erected with no overall masterplan, leading to a rather disjointed and disparate arrangement of facilities. Consequently, in 2011 John McAslan and Partners (see also page 196) were commissioned to create a cohesive campus with improved circulation and navigation for pupils and staff, and to maximise the space available. Barry's New College lies at the centre of these proposed plans and will be totally restored, with relandscaping of the main entrance to improve access and provide views of the Barry building.

The school will be celebrating its 400-year anniversary in 2019, by which time the impressive new masterplan will have been completed.

Above: *The New College lies at the heart of the campus, situated within 70 acres of grassland.*
Opposite: *The founder of Dulwich College, Edward Alleyn, is responsible for much of the school's archive, of which a number of volumes reside in the Masters' Library.*

Clapham Manor Primary School, SW4

The growing popularity of Clapham Manor Primary School in Clapham Old Town prompted the commission of a new extension, initially simply to provide extra classrooms. However, the vision of the architects de Rijke Marsh Morgan, working in close collaboration with the school governors and local authorities, resulted in a masterplan to transform the school by tackling deficiencies throughout the existing building as well as creating new space.

Completed in 2009, the four-storey extension is attached to the existing three-storey Victorian school through a glass atrium, which visually acts as a bridge between old and new and forms a dramatic school entrance. But it is the new wing that really catches the eye, with its multicoloured glass façade and brick-bond pattern detailing. Although striking, the new extension neither dominates nor is subservient to the old school building and the historic Odd Fellows Hall next door. The vibrant colour spectrum of the glass was chosen in close collaboration with the school's staff and pupils, and features reds and yellows on the Stonhouse Street side, with blues and greens on the side overlooking the playground. As daylight changes, the colours alter their levels of intensity, and reflections rippling across the façade add to the visual subtleties. The façade is inspired by post-war schools, which used glass curtain walls to create bright, airy teaching spaces.

The inventiveness of this façade extends to its interior wall, which intersperses pin boards that display the children's work with opaque and clear areas of glass arranged at different heights to provide children of all ages and adults with views to the outside. Unlike traditional school buildings, there are no corridors in this new wing. Instead, a central space leads off to the classrooms, creating a very open feel. The new wing has provided additional classrooms, a performance space and improved staff facilities. Outside there are a number of small 'pocket' garden areas as well as a playground.

With the striking design solution to provide extra space for the school, the architects have created an innovative learning environment that will adapt to future requirements while maintaining its visual acuity. It has been widely acclaimed and has won a number of awards, including Winner of the Civic Trust Award, 2010, as well as being shortlisted for the RIBA Stirling Prize the same year.

Above: *The school's staff and pupils helped choose the colour spectrum of the glass façade. On the interior of these walls, coloured pinboards where the children's work can be displayed are combined with clear and opaque areas of glass* (left).

This inspired play centre is situated in the eight-acre Kilburn Grange Park, and was completed in 2010 by Erect Architecture. The same year it won the International Children's Making Spaces Award, with children on the judging panel.

There could be no better validation for the architects, since the views of these children entirely matched their original concept for the building. They wanted to create a new type of play centre for children – one that would actively encourage them to develop new skills, engage with their environment and feel like it belonged to them. The concept of ownership of the built environment, particularly in relation to children, is important for instilling security and self-confidence while also encouraging the development of identity and creativity. During the course of this project, the architects actively involved local children in the design process by organising workshops to understand what they wanted from the centre, so the finished product was an accurate reflection of their needs.

The main activity building is timber framed, with a largely exposed structure, and is designed to make children feel like they are outdoors, playing among trees. Large internal columns made of tree trunks support the roof, and irregularly placed windows in the walls and roof allow light to filter through the beams, creating the effect of passing through a forest canopy.

The interior consists mainly of one large, open-plan play area, with a series of 'outdoor rooms' radiating from this with varying degrees of enclosure, each offering different exciting adventure opportunities. The children are encouraged to be outside and actively engage with their surroundings by exploring and fully

Opposite: *This timber-framed building with a largely exposed structure aims to create an interior space that gives children the feeling they are playing among trees. The use of recycled doors* (left) *is one of the elements that make this a sustainable construction.*

utilising the play areas available. These have been designed to be physically and mentally challenging, introducing an element of 'supervised risk' that is so important to development.

The whole building has been constructed with great emphasis on sustainability, and this extends to the biodiversity roof created by Bauder, which contains small plants that will eventually cover the whole surface, flowering at different times of the year and adding great aesthetic and environmental interest for the children.

This far-reaching project, winner of a RIBA Award, 2011, has already proved of enormous benefit to the local community, and due to its flexible and creative design, will be able to develop according to the needs of future generations of children.

The London Library, SW1

Victorian writer and historian Thomas Carlyle was one of a group of men who together founded the London Library in 1841 in direct competition with the British Library. Carlyle wanted to create an institution that would allow subscribers access to a national library in their own home, and was supported in his quest by a number of eminent and enlightened academics, including the politicians William Gladstone and the Earl of Clarendon, who became the Library's first President, and novelists William Makepeace Thackeray, Charles Dickens and George Eliot. Today, the London Library is the largest independent lending library in the world and houses over one million books. The library's founding principles include a stipulation that books should be stored on fully browsable, open-access shelves. When combined with the need to accommodate up to 8,000 new acquisitions a year, the library has to add approximately half a mile of extra shelving a year.

The library has occupied and expanded from its current home in St James's Square since 1845 and still houses many of its books in their original Victorian cast-iron bookshelves (sometimes referred to as 'bookstacks'). Since its beginnings, the library has had to expand into other buildings and has recently begun a four-phase regeneration and expansion project undertaken by Haworth Tompkins Architects (see also page 144), the first two stages of which are now complete.

The first stage, completed in 2007, entailed the remodelling of a disused 1970s office building fronting Mason's Yard, with the purpose of providing additional space to accommodate a much-needed conservation studio, staff areas and the all-important additional bookshelves. Although of little architectural merit, this building offered the opportunity to expand without moving the services off site, so freeing up space in the main library for further development. The design challenge was to find a strong contemporary language alongside the distinctive character of the library's architecture. The rather unexciting brick façade of the original block was remodelled with projecting windows, flush brickwork, black render and a glass ground-floor base. Inside, the building was stripped back to its concrete shell and left 'raw' for a textured look. Shiny black

bookshelves and minimal use of detailing make this interior calm and conducive to concentration, and new lavatories were designed in collaboration with the Turner-Prize-winning artist Martin Creed.

The second stage of work, in 2010, involved extending the library to provide 42 reader spaces as well as new designated rooms to hold the vast collections of art books, periodicals and publications of a wide range of societies. In addition, the interior design was updated, circulation and access throughout the library improved, the main Issue Hall was remodelled and further lavatories were installed, again designed by Martin Creed.

Today, the overwhelming feel of this library of many parts is one of contemporary detailing and design, yet it manages to complement the historic aspects of the building. The final two phases of work will include further expansion and new bookshelves, the creation of a 21st-century Reading Room, Members' Room and Terrace, and refurbishment of the first-floor Reading Room.

Above: *The London Library art room maintains the character of the traditional stacks, with an elegantly updated appearance.*

Peckham Library, SE15

Colourful and engaging are characteristics that are not traditionally associated with library buildings, but those are exactly the qualities Will Alsop (as Alsop and Störmer) created with the design for the new Peckham Library, opened in 2000.

The library is structured around an upside-down 'L' shape, with a prominent projection that provides a covered external space beneath. The projection is supported by slender columns arranged diagonally, creating a sense of dynamism, as if the building were walking. On the roof, large white letters spell out 'LIBRARY', and a giant red, sculptural element that houses a roof light juts over the edge. The rear façade of the building is covered with multicoloured glass panels, while the rest of the building is faced with a distinctive green, pre-patinated, copper-and-steel mesh (for security) and punctuated by small windows. This is a building that grabs the attention of passers-by and challenges preconceptions rather than sitting quietly within its setting.

At five storeys high, the library, part of a major regeneration programme in this area of South London, offers a great deal more than books. The first two floors house various council information and education services, with an office/interview 'pod' built in an open-tulip design and further mini, timber-clad pods that provide privacy during consultations. The library occupies the entire fourth floor.

Alsop located the library at this height to give the visitor a sense of entering a different world, having been on a 'journey' from the ground floor to the upper storeys. It was also a way of removing the reading areas from the noise at street level. The views across London extend to St Paul's Cathedral, the Tate Modern and the London Eye, and the library floor features three large pods, which stand on concrete legs and are also accessible from an upper gallery. These pods provide a soundproof children's activity centre, a meeting room that provides a flexible space for various types of gatherings, and an Afro-Caribbean area, which reflects the cultural dynamics of the district and is home to a large collection of literature and music.

This influential building has been a resounding success within the community since it opened in 2000, and in the same year it won the RIBA Stirling Prize for its design.

Above: *Three timber-clad pods standing on concrete legs are situated within the library, each with a separate purpose.*
Left: *The large white letters on top of the building clearly announce its purpose to the wider community.*

Hackney Empire
Phoenix Cinema
Hampstead Theatre
Royal Festival Hall
Wilton's Music Hall
LSO St Luke's
Camden Roundhouse
National Tennis Centre
Olympic Park
Greenwich Yacht Club
The Travellers Club
The Reform Club
St Pancras Chambers
Town Hall Hotel
St Martin's Lane Hotel

CULTURE AND RECREATION

'It is a source of constant fascination to me how a design brief between architect and the client, whether one individual, an institution or a business, comes to fruition. There are now many contemporary buildings in London directly responding to the world we live in now.'
Open House London visitor

London's reputation as a liveable city has long been associated with its wealth of impressive architecture for culture, leisure and sport. The exuberance of the capital's innumerable theatres, cinemas and concert halls, for example, reflects the rich diversity of London's cultural life: from the late-Victorian Hackney Empire to the Phoenix Cinema in Finchley – one of the oldest independent cinemas still operating in the United Kingdom – with its superb Art Deco detailing. Both of these buildings, now restored and updated, continue to play a significant role in the life of their communities, and are a source of great local pride.

Like other spaces for meeting and gathering, cultural and sporting venues have become a focus for regeneration throughout the capital. Contemporary architects have revitalised historic buildings that had become redundant or fallen into decline in order to adapt them for 21st-century use: the dilapidated 18th-century St Luke's Church was gutted and transformed into a new musical performance and education space for the London Symphony Orchestra; likewise, the redundant Bethnal Green Town Hall has been turned into an award-winning hotel and apartment building. Both projects have integrated key visible elements of the historic fabric alongside contemporary interventions. Similarly, the major refurbishment of the Royal Festival Hall, at the heart of the cultural complex on the South Bank, has enhanced the acoustics, comfort and facilities of this renowned building to recapture the spirit of the 1951 Festival of Britain for which it was constructed. The Greenwich Yacht Club buildings form part of the Greenwich Millennium Village development – a scheme intended to create a sustainable new community on the eastern side of the Greenwich Peninsula.

More recently, the 2012 London Olympic and Paralympic Games – the largest design and construction project in Europe – are the catalyst for the transformation of a once-decayed, largely industrial landscape in east London. The intention is to leave a lasting legacy of outstanding sporting facilities, alongside infrastructure, housing and green spaces in an area currently experiencing high levels of deprivation, to create places where people will want to live, work and play – and legacy was a key factor in London winning the Games. Reflecting the aim of creating the 'greenest' Games ever, sustainability was integrated into planning and design from the initial stages, with the commitment to create permanent structures only where they will have a long-term use after the Games, for example the Olympic Stadium, Aquatics Centre and Velodrome.

Hackney Empire, E8

Built in 1901 in only five months, the Hackney Empire remains one of the finest examples of late-Victorian variety palaces – a theatre dedicated to popular entertainment, such as music hall, burlesque and variety shows. Throughout its history, the venue has hosted some of the greatest names in show business, including Charlie Chaplin, Stan Laurel and Houdini; in the 1980s, it was one of the leading venues for the then up-and-coming, alternative-style stand-up comedians. As much as it is a defining venue in the world of variety entertainment, the Empire is also a significant feature on the Hackney skyline. The venue also plays a vital role in the life of the local community, and its modernisation by Tim Ronalds (see also page 192), completed in 2004, played a key role in the wider regeneration of this area of east London.

The building is the work of prolific architect Frank Matcham who, together with two colleagues, designed about 200 theatres and variety palaces in Britain. Commissioned by the young impresario Oswald Stoll, the Empire is now the only Matcham theatre surviving in its original use in London.

The Victorian façade indicates a building given over to exuberant entertainment, with its ornate domes, arched central balcony and statue of the Greek muse of music, Euterpe, set on a pedestal at the top of the building. The extravagance is amplified in the interior – first, in the resplendent Rococo-Baroque-style entrance foyer, with mosaic flooring and decorative tiled dados, and then, even more so, in the auditorium. Matcham embraced developing technologies during his build, and the theatre was noted for its central heating, 'air conditioning' (which was achieved through the use of a sliding roof), electric lighting and in-built projection box, which was located at the back of the dress circle and was used to show short films as a finale to the evening's entertainment; from 1915, the theatre also started to show films on Sundays.

The Empire's variety entertainment days ended in 1956; it later became the first commercial television studio in the country, and a bingo hall from 1963 to 1986. The same year, it was taken over by a group of actors and artists led by Roland Muldoon, who set up the Hackney New Variety Management Co. Ltd, and the charity Hackney Empire Preservation Trust, which returned it to being a variety

SAFETY CURTAIN

theatre. Today, it is once again a favourite entertainment destination.

In 2001, following allocation of Lottery and government regeneration funds, and with private funding, architect Tim Ronalds was commissioned to restore and refurbish the Empire. He aimed to adapt the theatre to modern requirements while retaining Matcham's architecture as far as possible. The programme included a new orchestra pit, an extension of the fly tower (with provision for counterweight flying), an expanded foyer and new lavatories.

The backstage area had to be entirely demolished and rebuilt. Ronalds also added the massive 'Hackney Empire' terracotta letters (6.4 metres/21 foot tall) to the exterior – a statement in keeping with the theatre's flamboyance.

Opposite: *Terracotta letters announce the building's identity.*
Above: *The refurbished theatre has remained faithful to Frank Matcham's original opulent architecture while adapting for modern requirements.*

Since 1985, the historic Phoenix Cinema has – unusually for a British cinema – been run by a charitable trust for the local community. It is also one of the oldest purpose-built, continually operating cinemas in the country, having stayed open to entertain Londoners throughout both World Wars.

The cinema was built in 1910 by Premier Electric Theatres, which went bankrupt before the opening. A private businessman stepped in and bought the building, and the East Finchley Picturedrome (as it was then called) opened for business in 1912, with its first film based on the ill-fated maiden voyage on the Titanic, which had taken place only a month earlier. In the 1920s, the name changed to the Coliseum, and in 1929 it became the first cinema in the area to screen a 'talkie' (an Al Jolson film called *The Singing Fool*).

The original building, designed by Stanley Birdwood, had a distinctive, barrel-vaulted ceiling, which still survives. However, the elaborate façade, featuring towers, domes and decorative detailing, was altered completely in the 1930s, when architects Howes and Jackman redesigned the exterior of the building in Art Deco style, adding glazed black tiles to a white façade – and a new canopy and neon sign, with the changed name of The Rex. Renowned cinema interior designers Mollo and Egan totally redesigned the inside of the building, with Art Deco wall panels and the introduction of a rich red, bronze and gold colour scheme – features that are retained to this day.

In 1975, the cinema changed hands and its name again, to the Phoenix, and started specialising in independent 'art house' films, but by the early 1980s the building was under threat of demolition. However, the community battled to preserve the cinema, forming the Phoenix Cinema Trust to buy and manage the business.

Since the take-over the building has been updated, with the addition of a new café-bar, the façade and neon signs have been restored, and the interior refurbished. The project, funded by the Heritage Lottery Fund, was completed in 2010. It is used regularly as a location for films, including *Nowhere Boy* (the biopic about John Lennon) and music videos.

Left: *The cinema features Art Deco wall panels and a rich colour scheme.*

Above: *Looking down from the first floor of the auditorium.*

The Hampstead Theatre's history stretches back over 50 years, and throughout that period plays by leading writers have been performed, including premieres of plays by Mike Leigh and Harold Pinter. The theatre's first home was in Moreland Hall, a church building next to the Everyman Cinema in Hampstead, north-west London, before it moved into a portable cabin in nearby Swiss Cottage, where the theatre was housed from 1962–2002 before moving to its new home in 2003.

The present Hampstead Theatre was the first freestanding theatre to be built in London since the National Theatre in 1975, and was designed specifically to support the theatre's tradition of fostering new playwrights. Designed by Bennetts Associates, who won a RIBA Award for the building the year it was opened, it is an important addition to the city's theatre landscape and is a simple, bold statement. It was also intended to be a catalyst for the wider regeneration of the Swiss Cottage area, and its glazed foyer provides views over a new park designed by Gustafson

Porter. The external appearance is one of simple, clean lines and geometric form, greatly enlivened through the architect's use of varied textured materials ranging from large expanses of glass, wood shuttering and slats to the tilting zinc drum that houses the auditorium.

Inside, the foyer is bright, airy and visually stimulating, created through the mix of internal structures, such as a galleried area and bridges that lead theatrically to the auditorium, sloping supporting columns and a polished floor. A café-bar adds to the friendly, sociable character of the building. The auditorium, which can seat 325 people, has a very flexible seating arrangement as well as a forestage that can be raised or lowered to allow for an orchestra pit. In addition, there is the smaller Michael Frayn Space, which can seat 80 people and is sometimes used for workshops.

The theatre is known not only for showcasing new writing talent but also for staging strong, dynamic plays that address contemporary issues.

The Royal Festival Hall was built as part of the Festival of Britain in 1951 – an event engineered to be a 'Tonic to the Nation' following the devastation of World War II. Dubbed 'the People's Palace', it has developed into a leading auditorium and greatly used public space.

In 1948, Labour Prime Minister Clement Attlee announced plans for a Festival of Britain, to be held on the South Bank of the river Thames on the site of the old Lion Brewery, between Waterloo Bridge and Hungerford Bridge. Central to the plans was the building of a permanent new concert hall that would be surrounded by temporary structures for the duration of the Festival. Sir Hugh Casson was appointed Director of Architecture for the Festival of Britain and he, in turn, appointed the young architects Leslie Martin, Peter Moro and Robert Matthew to design the Royal Festival Hall. The foundation stone was laid by Attlee in 1949, and just 18 months later a concert attended by King George VI and Queen Elizabeth (later known as The Queen Mother) marked the opening of the hall.

This was a bold landmark building. Intended to represent regeneration in the post-war years, it was an unashamedly Modernist statement, with its white stone and glass façades. Leslie Martin described the structure as 'an egg in a box', the curved 'egg' housing the auditorium and the 'box' the surrounding building space. The interior functions of the building are clearly expressed on the exterior, with the domed auditorium 'hovering' above the strongly horizontal planes of the façade, which give way to the light, glass-fronted foyers inside.

Over 8 million people flocked to the Festival, but as it came to an end the temporary structures were removed and the concert hall was left somewhat isolated on the South Bank until the 1960s, when further building took place. In 1964, foyers and terraces were added to overlook the river, and work soon began on the Queen Elizabeth Hall and Purcell Room (opened in 1967) and the Hayward Gallery (1968). Together with the Royal Festival Hall, these buildings make up the Southbank Centre – the largest single-run arts centre in the world.

An important change occurred to the Royal Festival Hall in 1983, when the Greater London Council implemented its 'open foyer' policy, encouraging the public to visit the building seven days a week and

Left: *The building's façade is a bold Modernist statement.*
Opposite: *Refurbishment of the concert hall aimed to reinstate the spirit of the 1951 building, while improving the acoustic and seating quality.*

putting on free events such as live concerts, jazz recitals and art exhibitions.

A major refurbishment programme, led by Allies and Morrison and completed in 2007, sought to reinstate the essence of the 1951 building and establish a new relationship with the South Bank riverside. The project involved remodelling the stage canopy and walls to improve the acoustics for performers and audience, and refurbishing seats, inserting air conditioning and new lighting for greater audience comfort. New performers' facilities and technical support were added, and foyers expanded by moving offices and shops outside into a new building next to the railway line. To recapture the spirit of the original building, the roof terraces were reopened and distinctive interior elements, such as the original 'Net and Ball' design for the carpets, were reintroduced. The project was shortlisted for the RIBA Stirling Prize, 2008.

The decorative doorway to Wilton's Music Hall – one of the oldest-surviving music halls in the world – barely hints at the gem hidden within. Originally, music halls were simply rooms attached to pubs where entertainment of a diverse nature was staged; the public either paid a small fee or the cost of their drinks was inflated. Over time, these rooms became more and more elaborate, although they continued to be accessed through pubs in order to avoid paying the high costs of a street frontage.

Built behind the Mahogany Bar owned by John Wilton, Wilton's Music Hall was designed by Jacob Maggs and opened in 1859. The bar was retained as the public entrance and the auditorium built behind five terraced houses. It replaced a much smaller hall used by Wilton since 1853. The pub changed hands a number of times over the years and suffered a serious fire in 1877, so the hall was largely rebuilt. During the refurbishment, a raked floor and a proscenium stage were added. The theatre had several landlords before it closed in the 1880s due to new fire regulations. Somewhat ironically, given its reputation as a place of bawdy entertainment, it was run as Methodist Mission until 1956, and then as a rag-sorting depot.

In the 1960s, the poet Sir John Betjeman (see also page 208) fronted a campaign to save Wilton's from demolition and it was finally bought by the Greater London Council and transferred to the Music Hall Trust. Performances began again in the grand old hall in 1999 after basic remedial works, including stage access, strengthening and making safe the balcony, fire-escape routes and basic electrical works and heating installation. These works were undertaken by volunteers from the local East End community.

The hall, which has remained virtually unchanged since the 1870s, is a simple configuration of a single auditorium with a balcony on three sides and a high stage. The balcony has a decorative papier mâché front (a popular material for building interiors in the 18th and 19th centuries), and is supported by slender, elegant barley-sugar columns made from cast iron and painted gold. Gold and duck-egg blue is the continuing colour theme across the walls and balcony, while the barrel-vaulted ceiling is pale yellow. In its heyday, it had a lantern skylight and was lit by gas chandeliers, with a further large chandelier of 300 gas jets and 27,000 cut crystals that generated so much heat that charring on the wooden rafters is still visible today.

Wilton's has suffered many long years of decay and neglect, but the building is now owned by the Wilton's Music Hall Trust, who are seeking funding for a project led by Tim Ronalds Architects (see also page 186) to stabilise and restore the building, including major works on the roofs, basement, soundproofing, ventilation and electrics. It is an atmospheric and evocative place and is a fascinating piece of 19th-century history as well as a vibrant centre for the performing arts.

Above: *The hall's decorative doorway opens into the entrance hall* (opposite, above). *Major restoration is underway to restore the building and its grand auditorium* (opposite, below) *to its original state.*

LSO St Luke's, EC1

The restored, early 18th-century church of St Luke's, on Old Street, is home to the London Symphony Orchestra's (LSO) community and music education programme, LSO Discovery, which helps people of all ages and abilities to engage with making music. It has become a lively arts centre for the local community and in particular offers opportunities and activities for those from disadvantaged areas of London.

The original church was commissioned in 1727 as part of the '50 New Churches Act', an Act of Parliament of 1711, passed with the aim of building 50 new churches for the expanding population of London, although only 12 were built. The two architects, John James and Nicholas Hawksmoor, were given a budget of £10,000. The church was consecrated in 1733, but because it was built on marshy ground it suffered a long history of repairs and subsidence. By 1959, following a particularly dry summer, the subsidence had reached such a dramatic level that the church was declared structurally unsound. The roof was removed, the organ was rehoused in St Giles Cripplegate and the interior was gutted.

The idea for housing the LSO Discovery programme at St Luke's was generated in the 1990s, partly because of the proximity of the dilapidated old church to LSO's home at the Barbican Centre. However, the building needed to undergo major renovation to make it safe and suitable for modern use. With the combined support of global finance firm UBS and Arts and Heritage Lottery funding, work began in 2000 to restore the building, supervised by architects Levitt Bernstein Associates, who juxtaposed historic and modern elements in a sensitive and cohesive way while retaining the integrity of each

component. The aim was to preserve the building's historic features while creating a working space that would meet the needs of contemporary performers and music educationalists. The brief from the LSO also involved using the whole space without subdividing it.

During the project, the exterior and many details of the church, such as the clock, were restored, a pavilion (which is used as a waiting area for performers before going on stage) was added in place of the original vestry, and the crypt was transformed to accommodate a restaurant, teaching and storage rooms and offices. But the real highlight of the interior is the huge, open central space, now called Jerwood Hall, which is large enough for

a full symphony orchestra plus a chorus to rehearse in and has excellent acoustics. The unplastered, rough walls (acoustically preferable to hard plaster) have been left as they were in the 18th century, and a contemporary steel structure of balconies and massive, tree-like columns supports the new roof. With its movable rostra and retractable seating, it is also an extremely versatile space.

LSO St Luke's has a constant programme of concerts, rehearsals, recording, teaching and various other activities taking place, including a series of free concerts outside the building in the summer during the City workers' lunch hour. This is a space that welcomes the public to participate in and enjoy music.

Opposite: *St Luke's church is home to the London Symphony Orchestra's community and education programme. The central space* (above), *now named Jerwood Hall, can house a full symphony orchestra plus chorus.*

Camden Roundhouse, NW1

The Camden Roundhouse, which has become a fixture of the London arts scene since its reconstruction was completed in 2006, gets its name from its origins as a Victorian 'roundhouse' – a circular building which housed a railway turntable engine shed.

Built in 1847 by celebrated architects Robert Dockray and George Stephenson (known for his work on the 'Rocket' locomotive with his son Robert), the 48m- (157ft-) diameter Roundhouse was deemed a prime feat of Victorian engineering. It served the London and North Western Railway for ten years before new engines became too large to be stationed there.

After a stint as a liquor warehouse, the Roundhouse passed through various hands but through the latter half of the 1900s has primarily been used as an arena for the arts; becoming a legendary music space in the 1960s and 1970s with The Doors and Jimi Hendrix performing there, and hosting iconic theatre productions, including Peter Brook's *The Tempest*.

The Roundhouse struggled with funding throughout the 1980s and 1990s but its fortunes improved after being bought by the Norman Trust, led by philanthropist Sir Torquil Norman in 1996 for £6 million. Sir Torquil established the Roundhouse Trust in 1998, which took on management of the building in 2000. With funding from the Arts Council, English Heritage and the Heritage Lottery Fund, renovation began in 2004, and was completed in 2006.

Architects John McAslan & Partners worked on the £29.7 million redevelopment, in conjunction with engineering company Buro Happold, creating a prime example of how an original building can be redeveloped through a combination of restoration and new build. Some of the original brickwork was exposed in the renovation and the main yellow brick building remains in place. A new steel and glass wing was added to the side of the Roundhouse – effectively curving round its circumference – to house the box office, administrative areas and a café/bar space as well as new circulation areas.

On entering the building, the visitor is immediately met by a steel staircase, which leads into the main performance area. On the same level as the concert hall, a wood-decked terrace provides a view over Camden.

In acknowledgement of the location's use as a site for music concerts throughout the year, the roof was given seven layers of soundproofing. The roof's original support of twenty-four cast-iron Doric columns remains in place – spaced at intervals reflecting where the engines would originally have sat.

As well as sound considerations, the architects looked closely at accessibility,

increasing the capacity of the main space so that it now holds 3,000 people standing and 1,700 seated. They also worked together with people with disabilities to ensure various issues of navigation around the building were addressed. As a consequence there are step-free routes throughout, handrails on all stairways, a colour scheme that clearly denotes which way to move around the building, and adequate space for wheelchairs, both in circulation routes and in lavatories.

Unsurprisingly, the Roundhouse has become a favourite of the local community, as well as with audience members. The Roundhouse Trust has targeted the local youth of Camden, founding a creative scheme for 11–25 year olds. With this programme in mind, the undercroft of the building was cleared of debris – although part of the turntable and sections of the early railway tracks were retained – and now functions as the Roundhouse Studios, a space for local youths to use for creative purposes.

Opposite: *The circular building gets its names from its origination as a Victorian 'roundhouse' – an engine shed.*
Above: *The original twenty-four cast-iron Doric columns supporting the roof remain in place.*

National Tennis Centre, SW15

The National Tennis Centre, completed in 2007, is the new home of British tennis and a centre for sporting excellence, providing the highest-specification training facilities in which to develop the skills of young British players. In 2002, the Lawn Tennis Association decided to relocate, owing to inadequate facilities at their existing Queen's Club HQ, and consolidate their operation on a single site – the Bank of England Sports Ground at Roehampton, south-west London. The complex is located in metropolitan open land, and the design responds to its setting, preserving the existing woodland and the 'open' character of the landscape.

One of the chief requirements in the design of this complex was to provide suitable housing for a number of different functions: indoor and outdoor tennis courts with grass, clay and acrylic surfaces; a gym and hydrotherapy pool; office spaces; sports medicine and sports science facilities; residential accommodation for students on training courses and a café.

The three buildings of the main complex, designed by Hopkins Architects and completed in 2007, are arranged around a central landscaped courtyard, the focus of which is a 250-year-old London plane tree. Some of the site is sloping,

so the main building is partially sunken into the landscape; in this way, it appears as a single-storey construction from the east, while providing sufficient height for the courts within. Again to overcome the sloping site, the outside courts were built as a series of terraces, linked through a ramp system. The indoor courts and player facilities are located on one side, and the residential areas on the other, the two being linked by a fabric-covered, glazed entrance pavilion. Next to the entrance is the world's first air-beam canopy (2010), designed by George Stowell in collaboration with engineers Airlight and

Opposite: *The fabric-covered glazed pavilion.*
Left: *An all-weather, air-beam canopy– the first of its kind – allows all-year-round use of the clay courts.*

Arup. This award-winning, all-weather structure enables the clay courts to be used year-round, and was designed as a prototype for other professional and community uses.

The façade is clad almost entirely in glass and cedar, and the sinuous lines of the arched roof create an impression of dynamism and movement, reflecting the physicality of sport. The reception area, with its large windows, affords views straight into the adjacent indoor courts, and leads to the café – a key meeting area for players, tutors, staff, public and parents. The entire interior is fully wheelchair accessible, including the lifts, which are spacious enough to accommodate a disabled tennis player sitting in a normal wheelchair while also pushing his or her special sports chair.

The building is designed to be highly energy efficient in terms of heating, lighting and ventilation, and is the largest indoor tennis facility in the United Kingdom to use underfloor heating – creating high levels of comfort but using minimal energy.

The end result is a world-class sports complex aimed to inspire young British players to become the international Grand Slam stars of the future.

Olympic Park, E20

Within the space of just five years, more than 46,000 people have helped create an entirely new quarter of London, with inspiring sporting venues and cutting-edge design.

The Olympic Delivery Authority (ODA) worked with world-class architectural and design teams to deliver designs for the main Olympic Park venues, infrastructure and parklands; including a new Olympic Stadium, Aquatics Centre, Velodrome, Handball Arena, and accommodation in the Athletes' Village, all in the heart of Stratford, east London, on a site that was formerly a largely derelict wasteland.

The venue designs, released in 2008 and 2009, combine flair with functionality. From the outset, they were all designed with legacy in mind. The Olympic Park needed to make an architectural statement in 2012. However, the ODA also wanted the Park to have a real sense of place after the Games, for local people to be proud of their new 'quarter' in London and for the venues and the Park to be as accessible as possible.

Design, innovation and creativity lie at the heart of the project. The approach has been to ensure these qualities are central at every stage – from planning and procurement through to construction. The designs for the Olympic Park have redefined this part of the city and the east London skyline.

Inclusive design was also at the heart of the process throughout. The sporting venues, the Athletes' Village, new transport services, supporting facilities and the Park itself are accessible to people with a wide range of disabilities. The project set an excellent standard of accessibility for disabled people, older people and families with children, which will set a benchmark and act as an inspiration.

As well as the firms contracted to design and build the venues, the success of the project was achieved with contributions from a range of different stakeholders, from community groups through to statutory bodies, notably partners in the design community – including the Commission for Architecture and the Built Environment, the Royal Institute of British Architects, the Landscape Institute, the local Boroughs, the Greater London Authority, the London Development

Agency and Design for London – all whose input was invaluable in helping to shape the final designs.

Community engagement was another key element to the project, and intense public interest in the development led the ODA to host over 250,000 visitors on bus tours throughout the build programme, with Open House London being the ODA's biggest annual event to open up the Park to the public to come and see the development for themselves .

The London 2012 Olympic and Paralympic Games have given an opportunity to show everything that is great about London and the United Kingdom. That includes the quality and inventiveness of British architecture, design, construction and engineering, all delivered on time and within budget.

The venues and Park have now become a new place for generations of Londoners, and a permanent reminder of the Olympic and Paralympic Games in 2012.

Above: *The curved roof of the Olympic Velodrome, a new facility for cycling in east London.*

Overleaf: *The Olympic Park, viewed North to South, almost complete in early 2012.*

The striking Greenwich Yacht Club building on Peartree Wharf sits alongside the New Millennium Village on the Greenwich Peninsula, south-east London. It was the first river-based recreational facility established in the development, and formed part of the overall regeneration of the site of the former East Greenwich Gas Works.

The Greenwich Yacht Club has a longstanding history in this area. Formed in 1908 by a small group of Thames watermen and river workers, their first clubhouse was a beached Thames sailing barge moored not far from the current building, followed by a hut on the Mudlarks Way beach. Later, the clubhouse was moved to a building on Riverway. However, since this location formed part of the planned construction site for the Millennium Dome (now the O2 Arena), the Yacht Club needed to move again and was compensated with a brand new clubhouse, teaching rooms and a café by English Partnerships (now part of the Homes and Community Agency), the government agency that owned the Dome site. Architects Frankl and Luty were commissioned to design the new facilities, which were opened in 2000.

The current clubhouse, which is the social focus of the Yacht Club, is a two-storey glass structure with zinc, aluminium and green oak cladding and a zinc roof. Built on an existing jetty in the river Thames, it has uninterrupted views of the river and waterfront, including the Thames Barrier and the O2 Arena. The exterior is enlivened by metal stairways, walkways and balconies, which free up interior space, and a large terrace, which overlooks the river. Inside, the clubhouse has a boat-like feel, not only because it is surrounded by water, but also because of the construction materials used – the walls feature exposed steel and timber cladding and the window frames and the floors of the main rooms are made of pine.

Today, Greenwich Yacht Club has over 400 members, and now it has its new facilities the club plans to expand its membership to accommodate more sailing and boating enthusiasts.

Left: *The two-storey glass structure stands on an existing jetty in the Thames.*

Above: *The library, which was the original home of the London Library (p 180–181), features a recreation of the Bassae Frieze.*

Established in 1819, following the Napoleonic Wars, the Travellers Club is the oldest of the Pall Mall clubs. The aim of its principal founder, Lord Castlereagh, was to provide a civilised social setting where gentlemen who had travelled abroad could entertain distinguished foreign visitors, and it remains a gentlemen-only club. Some of its eminent members include various former prime ministers, such as the 1st Duke of Wellington, Stanley Baldwin and George Canning. Fictional characters in Graham Greene's novels also flit in and out of the rooms at the club.

After outgrowing its previous premises at 49 Pall Mall, the Travellers Club commissioned architect Sir Charles Barry – who was later involved in the new Houses of Parliament rebuild and designed the Reform Club next door (see page 206) – to create a purpose-built building, which was opened at 106 Pall Mall in 1832. Having just returned from Italy, Barry was influenced by Renaissance architecture and took inspiration for his design of the façade from Raphael's Palazzo Pandolfini in Florence (1515–20), and the garden façade shows the influence of Venetian architecture. The tower to Barry's design was added in 1842.

The interior is more ornate than the exterior. Many of the principal rooms still retain their original fixtures and fittings, including mahogany furniture and brass light fittings designed by Barry. The library is perhaps the most important room in the building, as it was the original home of the London Library (see pages 180–81). Over two thirds of the books here are related to travel, and the room is also noted for its recreation of the 5th-century Greek Bassae Frieze (currently in the British Museum and excavated by architect and Club member C. R. Cockerell) by Scottish sculptor John Henning (1771–1851) and his son, John.

This is a building full of character and tradition and has been altered little during its history. In recent years, the Bramall Room on the lower-ground floor (where female guests are welcome) has been developed to provide access to Carlton Gardens, but very sympathetically and in keeping with the rest of the interior.

The Reform Club originated in the 19th century, following the passing of the Great Reform Act of 1832, for which all club members had to pledge support. Both Radicals and members of the Whig party, which included William Gladstone and Lord Palmerston, created the club as a centre for their political activities, and it became the headquarters of the new Liberal party. Since the 1920s, the club has had no affiliations with any particular political party and its prime function is now social. It was among the first of the gentlemen's clubs to admit female members, in 1981.

The palatial building on Pall Mall, home to the Reform Club since 1841, is an architectural masterpiece built by Sir Charles Barry, who also designed the adjacent Travellers Club (see page 205) and the Houses of Parliament. Strongly resembling Michelangelo's Palazzo Farnese in Rome (1589), the façade displays a style of architecture known as Italian Palazzo, or Renaissance Revival, which exhibits a range of different characteristics loosely based on Italian classical architecture (rather than the Regency style, which was prevalent at the time). The style was relatively new to London, but quickly became a fashionable model for many prestigious buildings, including banks, private clubs and even private homes in London and beyond. The Pall Mall façade is symmetrical in design, with pedimented windows on the first floor and a richly carved frieze above. At the top of the façade is a projecting cornice that features carvings of emblems associated with the United Kingdom – the rose, the shamrock and the thistle, as well as dolphins, possibly denoting the island status of the country.

The inside of the building is considerably more opulent than the exterior: a set of stairs brings the visitor into a magnificent square atrium, or central court, which reaches the full height of the building and has a faceted glass roof that reflects and diffuses light in all directions. Yellow marble Corinthian columns surround the square at ground- and first-floor levels, and a colourful mosaic pavement bears an Etruscan design, making the space feel like an Italian courtyard. Large portraits of important Whigs and Radicals and huge mirrors adorn the walls, the latter making the building seem grander and even more spacious than it actually is. The gilded ceilings and frequent use of the letter 'R' in the decorative detailing throughout the club further add to the luxurious nature of this building. The Morning Room on the lower floor has a half-size copy of the Parthenon frieze around the walls.

Distinguished past 'Reformers' include novelists Henry James, H. G. Wells, William Makepeace Thackeray and J. M. Barrie, as

well as former prime ministers Sir Winston Churchill and David Lloyd George (who both resigned over the blackballing of a friend from the club). In Jules Verne's classic novel *Around the World in 80 Days*, published in 1873, it was where Phileas Fogg began and ended his global voyage, having made a bet with other Reform Club members. Today there are 2,700 members from a wide spectrum of professions.

Opposite: *Italian classical architecture is invoked in the Club's façade.*
Above: *The central atrium, with its faceted glass roof.*

St Pancras Chambers, NW1

The British poet Sir John Betjeman (1906–84, see also page 192) described this extraordinary building as 'too beautiful and too romantic to survive', yet it was largely through his efforts that it was awarded a Grade I listing in 1967, which saved it from demolition.

The building dates to 1865, when the Midland Railway ran a competition to design a hotel adjacent to the 'soon to open' St Pancras Railway Station. Sir George Gilbert Scott, who had previously worked on the Foreign Office and India Office (see page 72), won the commission in 1866 with a grand design for a hotel twice the size of the original specifications. His finished hotel, which opened in 1876 and was called the Midland Grand, is widely considered to be one of the finest examples of Victorian Gothic architecture. Scott took inspiration from medieval Gothic buildings all over Europe, most notably the cloth halls of northern France and Flanders. The red brick and stone of the façade were sourced in the Midlands.

Scott's grand double staircase is one of the most compelling elements of the interior, with its wrought-iron balustrading, original gas-light fittings and exceptional width, designed to allow two ladies wearing bustles to pass each other in comfort. Above it is a tremendous vaulted ceiling painted with stars and heraldic references to the Great Midland Railway. The interior features gold-leaf decorative detailing in the grandest rooms and elaborate fireplaces, many of which were constructed from different-coloured marble. Typically of the time, the bedrooms (of which there were more than 300) did not have *en suite* facilities, but unusually for a 19th-century hotel it did have flushing lavatories. The hotel also incorporated other innovations, such as the hydraulic 'ascending rooms' (lifts), which

served the first four floors; revolving doors, which were highly novel at the time; and an ingenious new electric-bell system so the guests could summon room service.

In 1922, the hotel was taken over by the London, Midland and Scottish Railway, and then closed in 1935 due to high running costs and facilities that had by that time become outdated. It was renamed the St Pancras Chambers and taken over by British Rail, to be used as their offices. During this period, much of the gold leaf and other decorative features were boarded up or painted over.

In the 1980s, the building was closed for many years after failing fire-safety regulations tests. However, the station was revamped and reopened in 2007, with St Pancras International replacing Waterloo as the terminus for Eurostar services and the addition of a new high-speed rail link across southern England.

Opposite: *Sir George Gilbert Scott's building is deemed to be one of the finest examples of Victorian Gothic architecture.* Left: *The distinctive double staircase features wrought-iron balustrades and original gas-light fittings.*

Property developers Manhattan Loft Corporation, in conjunction with London and Continental Railways, the conservation specialists Richard Griffiths Architects and RHWL Architects, undertook a major restoration of St Pancras Chambers, returning it to a hotel on the lower floors and the new west wing of the station, and creating 67 private apartments on the upper floors, including the landmark clock tower. Much of the original decoration was restored, and mezzanine galleries were added to the large Victorian rooms to provide further space. The St Pancras

Renaissance Hotel had its grand opening in 2011 (exactly 135 years after the building originally opened as the Midland Hotel).

St Pancras train station was designed in 1863 by William Barlow and constructed 1866–68, becoming the largest enclosed space in the world, with the train shed spanning 74 metres (243 feet). Restoration work completed in 2007 as part of a master plan by Foster and Partners (see also pages 16, 36, 52, 58, 80), and later Alistair Lansley, has extended and refurbished the station, with the shed reglazed and repainted its intended sky blue.

This imposing hotel converted from a former town hall in the centre of the East End has retained its historic character despite a recent complete refurbishment and regeneration. Its roots can be traced to the start of the 20th century, when the local council held a competition to design a town hall for Bethnal Green. This area of London was experiencing substantial growth at the time, and the new building needed to accommodate the increasing requirements of the council while expressing its status and ambition.

Opened in 1910 by Charles Fox, the Mayor of Bethnal Green, the finished Town Hall, designed by Percy Robinson with W. Alban Jones, had an Italianate-style façade, decorated with sculptures by Henry Poole, and a distinctive central tower with cupola. The interiors were equally impressive, particularly the entrance hall, with its veined marble floor and walls and grand staircase. Many of the walls had oak wainscoting, while the floors were of polished teak. Fine decorative plasterwork and leaded windows with stained-glass panels narrating local legends added to the rich decoration of the building.

By the 1930s, the council had outgrown the Town Hall and a substantial extension, designed by E. P. C. Monson, was added. Like the original building, the façade of the extension was constructed from Portland stone for continuity, but it was more austere in nature and in the neo-classical style, which nonetheless married well with the existing façade. The extension's interior is decorated in the Art Deco style, with a marble-lined entrance hall, an inlaid marble floor, brass fittings and a sensitive use of wood panelling (walnut in the Council Chamber and mahogany in the Mayoral Office). The imposing

staircase was lined with travertine and the square columns and pilasters were faced in brown-grey marble.

Weathering World War II relatively unharmed, the Town Hall remained in active council duty until the 1980s, when the final few remaining offices were moved to Tower Hamlets. For some time, the building was used as a film location – both Keira Knightley and Emma Thompson have filmed there – but over the years the interiors began to suffer from neglect, until 2007, when Singapore lawyer-turned-hotelier Peng Loh bought the building and set about converting it to a hotel with the help of Rare Architecture.

The aim was to modernise the building and add the extra space required for a luxury hotel, without losing any of the atmosphere and richness. The original features, including the grand marble staircases and public rooms, such as the Council Chamber, have been carefully restored to maintain their former grandeur, while the original utilitarian office spaces (now the guest bedrooms) have been transformed with contemporary design details. Wood, marble and glass have been used consistently throughout for maximum aesthetic effect, and specially commissioned paintings and sculptures by up-and-coming artists from this creative hub of London adorn the public spaces. The rear façade has a distinctive, laser-cut aluminium 'veil' with a pattern inspired by the original Art Deco metal ornament in the Council Chamber.

The Town Hall was opened as a hotel and apartments in spring 2010, and with its 98 rooms is a fine example of a historic building being sympathetically re-engineered for a new role. In 2011, it was winner of the RICS Building Conservation Award and a RIBA London Award.

Opposite: *The original features of the hotel, such as the grand marble staircases, have been carefully restored.*

St Martin's Lane Hotel, which occupies former offices dating from the 1960s, can be found deep in the heart of vibrant Covent Garden – one of the liveliest areas in London, surrounded by many West End theatres and with the buzz of a place that never sleeps.

The hotel provides a sensory experience from the moment the guests enter through the luminescent yellow-glass revolving doors – the tallest of their kind in London. Height, space and drama are continuing themes in the extravagant foyer. It is unsurprising, therefore, that the philosophy behind the building is 'hotel as theatre'.

Opened in 1999, this was the first hotel owned by the American Morgans Hotel Group in England, and was the creation of contemporary French designer Philippe Starck. Morgans Hotel Group developed its first property (known as Morgans) in 1984 on Madison Avenue, New York, and is credited with introducing the now extremely popular 'boutique hotel' concept, in which contemporary design plays a key role, along with personalised service. Another requisite is that boutique hotels provide a unique environment that separates them from the homogeneity of chain hotels, and in this respect St Martin's is a typical example.

Starck has created a theatrical and

Left: *The entrance to the hotel, with its luminescent yellow-glass revolving doors, indicates the dramatic design within* (opposite).

luxurious interior throughout, that draws on a range of influences, from the Baroque to the contemporary, playing on the distortion of proportions, such as the enormous doors and vertiginous foyer, with its oversized columns and the alignment of brilliant colours and textures. This is most evident in the angled, fluorescent-yellow niches in the foyer and the Portuguese limestone floors, along with dramatic lighting. Starck continued his use of intense colours through to the bedrooms, which also include his furniture designs. Full floor-to-ceiling windows and interactive lighting in a spectrum of colours, which can be altered by guests to suit their current mood, add to the flamboyant ambience.

Hotels {213}

ART DECO A style of design and architecture, which peaked in popularity in the 1930s, characterised by geometrical shapes and linear, symmetrical designs and the use of streamlined motifs.

ART NOUVEAU A style of art and architecture, predominantly of the 1890s, characterised by flowing, asymmetrical lines and curves and stylised natural forms, such as flowers and leaves.

ARTS AND CRAFTS A design movement that became popular in the late 19th century, particularly in Britain, drawing on medieval styles of decoration and traditional craftsmanship.

ATRIUM (pl. atria) A central, often glass-roofed hall that extends through several storeys of a building.

BAROQUE A style of architecture in Europe, prevalent from the late 16th to the early 18th century, characterised by extensive ornamentation.

BARREL-VAULTED CEILING An arched ceiling in the form of a half-cylinder.

BREAKOUT AREA An informal space in an office building where staff can meet, relax and socialise.

BRUTALISM/NEW BRUTALISM An austere architectural style of the 20th century, characterised by stark geometric forms and undressed concrete.

CANTILEVERED A structure that is fixed at one end only and projects outwards beyond its support.

CAPITAL The upper part of a column or pilaster.

CHINOISERIE A style of art based on Chinese motifs. Its popularity peaked in the middle of the 18th century.

CLADDING The material used for the outside of a building.

CLASSICAL A style of architecture derived from ancient Greek or Roman architecture and which inspired many other styles after the Renaissance. See also Neo-classical.

COMPETITION A process whereby a sponsor, company or body that plans to build a new building asks architects to submit proposed designs. The winning design is usually chosen by an independent panel or jury. Architecture competitions can be open to all, limited to groups, or on an invitation-only basis.

CORINTHIAN COLUMN A style of column, taken from Greek classical architecture, characterised by a bell-shaped capital intricately carved with acanthus leaves or other foliage and flowers and (usually) a fluted vertical shaft. See also Ionic and Doric column.

CURTAIN WALL A non-load-bearing external wall attached to a building.

DORIC COLUMN A classical Greek-style column, with no base, a fluted vertical shaft and a smooth capital that flares from the column to join a square abacus (the flat slab that forms the uppermost part of the capital). See also Corinthian and Ionic column.

DORMER WINDOW A vertical window that projects from a sloping roof, unlike a roof light, which is flush with the surface of the roof.

ETFE A type of plastic noted for its strength and resistance to corrosion, and used to cover the outside of buildings or for roofs.

EXOSKELETON A hard frame on the outside of a building that provides the structure with greater stability.

FAÇADE The face of a building, usually the main front.

FAN-VAULTED CEILING A feature of Gothic architecture, characterised by ribs that emerge from the top of a capital and radiate outwards, like a fan.

FIBONACCI SEQUENCE A set of numbers that starts with a one or a zero, followed by a one, proceeding on the rule that each number (called a Fibonacci number) is equal to the sum of the preceding two numbers. Fibonacci numbers are often found in patterns or shapes in nature.

FLY TOWER The large space above a stage where a system of rigging, pulleys and other devices used to move theatre equipment (such as scenery and lighting) around the stage are stored.

FUNCTIONALISM The theory of design prevalent in the 20th century that the design of a building ought to be determined by its use. Danish Functionalism, which was popular in the 1960s, kept ornamentation to a minimum and was characterized by straight angles, flat roofs and untreated concrete.

GOTHIC A style of architecture that flourished in Western Europe between the 12th and 16th centuries, characterised by the pointed arch, the ribbed vault and the flying buttress.

GREEN ROOF A roof that is covered with plants, often sedum. It absorbs excess water, helping prevent flash flooding, provides an additional layer of insulation and is good for encouraging wildlife.

HIGH TECH A style of architecture of the 1970s, which adopted elements of high-tech industry and technology into building design.

HIGH-PERFORMANCE GLAZING – Glass with a special coating that controls the amount of sunlight transmitted through it, preventing heat loss in winter and heat gain in summer.

IONIC COLUMN A style of column, taken from Greek classical architecture, characterised by an elegant, fluted vertical shaft and capital with scroll-like ornamentation. See also Corinthian and Doric.

ITALIANATE A style of architecture, popular in Britain and other parts of the world in the 19th century, based on 16th-century Italian Renaissance architecture.

ITALIANATE RENAISSANCE A classical style of architecture revived and developed by Venetian architect Andrea Palladio (1508–80), whose designs for villas and palaces influenced English architecture in the 17th and 18th centuries.

LANCET WINDOWS Acutely pointed, arched windows typical of the Gothic style.

LIGHTWELL An open area or shaft in the centre of a building that allows light through.

LISTED BUILDING A building officially recognised as having special architectural or historical interest and therefore protected from demolition or alteration without special permission being granted. There are different levels of grading, the highest being Grade I.

MODERNISM A groundbreaking 20th-century architectural movement pioneered by Mies van der Rohe, Le Corbusier and Frank Lloyd Wright among others, characterised by undecorated forms, straight lines and use of glass, steel and reinforced concrete.

NEO-CLASSICAL An architectural style of the mid-18th and 19th centuries that recalls the architecture of classical Greece and the Renaissance.

NEO-CLASSICAL PALLADIAN A neo-classical style of architecture that took its inspiration from the 16th-century Venetian architect Andrea Palladio (1508–80).

NEW BRUTALISM see Brutalism.

PARAPET A low wall or railing along the edge of a balcony or roof.

PEDIMENT The triangular section above a door or window, as found in classical, Renaissance and neo-classical architecture, and typically supported by columns.

PHOTOVOLTAIC PANELS A system of interconnected and packaged cells that convert sunlight into electricity, generally found on roofs.

PILASTER A shallow, rectangular column attached to the face of a wall.

PITCHED ROOF A roof that slopes steeply.

PORTAL An entrance way or doorway, particularly one that is grand and imposing.

PORTICO An external entrance to a building, covered with a roof and often supported by columns or pillars.

PORTLAND STONE An elegant white stone from Dorset, often used for large public buildings and grand residential properties, for example Buckingham Palace.

PRE-RAPHAELITE BROTHERHOOD A group of English painters and writers, including Rossetti, Holman Hunt and Millais, founded in 1848 to challenge conventional academic painting and revive the direct, personal experience of nature.

PROSCENIUM STAGE A stage where the audience sits on one side only and views the performance through a proscenium (an arch or opening).

RAINWATER-HARVESTING SYSTEM A recycling system that collects rainwater from the roof during wet weather and then filters and pumps it back into some or all of the water supply. The main benefits are that it offsets or replaces mains supply use, and can reduce storm-water runoff, making flooding less likely.

RAKED A floor that slopes towards the rear of the room or stage.

RENAISSANCE A style of architecture in Europe between the early 15th and early 17th centuries, characterised by symmetry and an emphasis on geometry and proportion, as in architecture of classical antiquity.

RENAISSANCE REVIVAL Refers to many 19th-century architectural revival styles, primarily those with Italian or French influence.

RIBA The Royal Institute of British Architects, founded in 1834 and a professional body for architects in the UK.

RIBA AWARDS A collection of prizes awarded by RIBA for great architecture, including the RIBA Stirling Prize (the most prestigious), the Lubetkin Prize, the Stephen Lawrence Prize and various medals.

RIB-VAULTED CEILING A feature of Gothic architecture, similar to a barrel-vaulted ceiling (see page 214) but with intersections (ribs), usually made of stone and carved for decoration, that link the barrel vaults.

ROCOCO A style of architecture and decoration that originated in Paris in the 18th century, characterised by ornate, graceful, florid ornamentation and often-asymmetrical motifs.

ROMANESQUE A style of architecture prevalent in western and southern Europe between the 9th and 12th centuries, characterised by rounded arches, groin vaults, thick walls and restrained use of ornamentation.

ROOF LIGHT Also known as a skylight, this is a window placed in a roof or ceiling that admits daylight into a building. Unlike a dormer window (see page 214), a roof light is flush with the roof surface.

ROTUNDA A building or room that has a circular plan, often with a dome.

SHARED OWNERSHIP Also known as part-shared housing, this is a form of house purchase where the purchaser buys a proportion of the dwelling (between 25 and 75 per cent), usually from the local authority or housing association, and rents the rest.

SLOT WINDOW A long, narrow horizontal window, sometimes used to 'frame' external views.

TENSILE FABRIC A material used in architectural structures, usually roofs. It can economically and attractively span large distances, creating intriguing three-dimensional effects, and allows light through. It is ideal for spanning the gap between two buildings.

TOP-LIGHTING A natural light source that enters a room from above, for example through a glass roof or roof light.

TRAVERTINE A form of limestone (in white, tan and cream) that is deposited by mineral springs and used as a building material.

UPSTAND A barrier used to prevent water from penetrating a flat roof or roof light.

VICTORIAN GOTHIC Also known as Gothic revival, or neo-Gothic, this style of architecture was popular between the late 18th and late 19th centuries and emulated the Gothic style (see page 215).

VITROLITE An opaque coloured glass used for tiling and façades of buildings from the 1920s to 1950s.

Some (but not all) of the 100 buildings featured in this book may be open for the Open House London annual event in September each year, and the full programme listings should be checked at www.openhouselondon.org.uk, available from mid-August.

The following buildings may also be open to the public throughout the year or on certain days. Areas accessible to the public may be limited or vary during the year, and an admission fee may be payable. Details and conditions of access MUST be checked in advance before you embark on your visit.

LONDON AT WORK
Crossness Engines House
Trinity Buoy Wharf / Container City

GOVERNANCE AND POWER
Barking Town Hall
City Hall
Guildhall
Royal Courts of Justice
The UK Supreme Court (formerly the Middlesex Guildhall)

LONDON AT HOME
2 Willow Road
BedZED
Leighton House

COMMUNITY, LEARNING AND STUDIOS
Bevis Marks Synagogue
Central Saint Martins College of Art & Design
Coin Street Neighbourhood Centre
Jerwood Space (Gallery)
Kentish Town Health Centre
Lumen United Reformed Church and Café
New Heart for Bow Project at St Paul's Old Ford
Peckham Library

St Martins-in-the-Fields
The Waldron Health Centre, Lewisham

CULTURE AND RECREATION
Hackney Empire
Hampstead Theatre
LSO St Luke's, UBS & LSO Music Education Centre
Phoenix Cinema
Roundhouse
Royal Festival Hall
St Martin's Lane Hotel
St Pancras Renaissance Hotel
Town Hall Hotel & Apartments
Wilton's Music Hall

For more information about the Open House London Annual Event and its buildings every year, visit www.openhouselondon.org.uk. To find out more about Open-City, the organisation behind Open House London, visit www.open-city.org.uk.

Index

Acknowledgements

Open House London first made its appearance 20 years ago and since that time it has become such a great success only through the efforts of thousands of individuals. Space does not allow me to personally name and thank all those people who have helped and contributed, freely giving their support, time and energy, without which this incredible event, now an annual highlight of London's cultural calendar, would simply not happen.

However, there are many key groups of people to whom the event is very much indebted. These include the home owners and building owners/representatives, architects and other built environment professionals, and volunteer guides and stewards who give up their time during Open House London to ensure that every participant can experience and enjoy it to the full.

In addition, I would also like to thank the many sponsors and supporters over the years, from the London local authorities to private companies, individual donors and curators, to institutions, organisations and companies such as BBC London, the British Council for Offices, British Land, Derwent London, Hammerson, Greater London Authority, ING Media, Institution of Civil Engineers, Landscape Institute, Maggie's Centres, Margaret Howell, Olympic Delivery Authority, Royal Institute of British Architects, The Architects' Journal, VIEW Pictures, Woobius and 4D Modelshop. And also to Robert Elms, Maxwell Hutchinson and Jason Badrock. And a very special thank you to Ken Allinson.

I would also like to acknowledge and recognise the input of all the dedicated Trustees, staff, volunteers and interns from within the organisation, and our supporters at large externally, who all contribute so much to the success of Open-City and its numerous initiatives.

I would specifically like to thank those below who have been our core Open House London team over the years who work tirelessly on all the preparations, encourage everyone to take part, and keep calm and smiling under pressure:

Jason Ahmed
Liz Antcliffe
David Attwood
Sebastian Avendano
Helen Baehr
Georgina Baker
Frank Beswick
Alasdair Bethley
Amanda Birch
Eleanor Campion
June Cannon
Adrianna Carroll-Battaglino
Hilary Clarke
Becky Coletto
Nick Cooney
John Cunningham
Jo Darke
Judith Davies
Nick Delaney
Fabian Draeger
Deborah Eker
Eke Elan
Jo Fells
Jean Fisker
Wendy Forrest
Catherine Foster
Nick Foster
Blanca Garay
Pam Gray
Bill Green
Martin Hartmann
Wayne Head
Des Hickey
Jeni Hoskin

James Hulme
Julia Hum
Rob Hurn
Alan Jacobs
Manon Janssens
Nicky Kemp
Robin Key
Hilary Kidd
Kit Lam
Julie Leonard
Marion Lesage
Ewa Lukaszczykiewicz
Hanne Lund
Fiona MacDonald
Emily Mann
Gayle Markovitz
Cecile Menom
Will Mesher
Gemma Mills
Richard Morgan
Elizabeth Nokes
Benedict O'Looney
Megan Phillips
Yvonne Pines
Richard Purver
Rosemary Read
Caroline Regan
Leonora Robinson
Stuart Rock
Hiromi Sasaki
Francesca Scoones
Stephen Senior
Kathy Slack
Catherine Smith
Grant Smith
Lucien Smith
Nicolette Spera
Andrew Stone
Fenella Stone
Miriam Sullivan
Elaine Tandoh
Suzanne Tarlin
Anne Thomas
Paul Thornton

Lucy Townsend
Helen Tsoi
Kelly van Cotthem
Robert van Helvoort
Miranda Westwood
Tom Westwood
Michael Whitaker
Lucietta Williams
Will Wimshurst
Muriel Wilson
Sarah Yates
Suzie Zuber

Thanks to Sarah Yates and Jeni Hoskin for providing such excellent assistance, ideas and help without which this publication would not have stayed on track.

Hannah Knowles at Ebury Press has worked with great commitment and enthusiasm for Open House, from conception to end product. Thanks also to Polly Boyd, Tamsin Pickeral, David Rowley and all the staff at Ebury Press for making this book a reality.

A special thank you to all those building owners and representatives, and architects, who have offered so much help and support in the production of this book.

It goes without saying that we have made every effort to ensure that all information is factually accurate but that of course where possible any errors will be corrected in subsequent editions.

Photographic Acknowledgements

Every effort has been made to contact all copyright holders. Any omissions or errors that may have occurred are inadvertent and will be addressed if notification is sent to the publisher.

LONDON AT WORK

p 10 (from top to bottom): © Grant Smith / View Pictures; reproduced by kind permission of the Crossness Engines Trust; © Adam Jacobs / Derwent London; © Nick Cooney; p 12 © David Borland / View Pictures; p 13 © Anne-Marie Briscombe; p 14 © Lee Mawdsley / Derwent London; p 15 © Adam Jacobs / Derwent London; p 16 & 17 © Grant Smith / View Pictures; p 18 & 19 © Grant Smith; p 20 & 21 © Simon Upton; p 23 © Nick Delaney; p 24 © Simon Upton; p 25 © Grant Smith; p 26 © Richard Brine; p 27 © Nick Cooney; p 28 & 29 © Steve Cadman / TfL; p 30 & 31 Congress House © James Brittain / View Pictures; p 32–33 © The Imagination Group Limited; p 34 © Hufton + Crow / View Pictures; p 35 top © Paul Riddle / View Pictures; bottom © Francesca Vezzani; p 36 © Grant Smith / View Pictures; p 37 © Chris Hollick; p 38 © Chris Gascoigne / View Pictures; p 38–39 © Simon Upton; p 40 © Chris Gascoigne / View Pictures; p 41 © Peter Cook / View Pictures; p 42 © Anthony Weller / View Pictures; p 43 © Hufton + Crow / View Pictures; p 44 © Anthony Weller / View Pictures; p 45 (both images) © Peter Cook; p 47 reproduced by kind permission of the Crossness Engines Trust; p 48–49 © Simon Upton

GOVERNANCE AND POWER

p 50 (from top to bottom): © Anthony Weller; © Royal College of Physicians; © Hanne Lund; © Edwin Jones; p 52 & 53 © Simon Upton; p 54 & 55 Michael C. McAleenan; p 57 © Hanne Lund; p 59 © Dennis Gilbert / View Pictures; p 60 © Anthony Weller / View Pictures; p 61 © Crown Copyright; p 62 © Simon Upton; p 64 © Paul Farmer; p 65 © Crown Copyright; p 66 & 67 © Anthony Weller / View Pictures; p 68 © Logan MacDougall Pope / View Pictures; p 69 © Sean Clarkson; p 70 & 71 © Bank of England; p 73 & 74 © Eugenia Ziranova; p 76, 77, 78 © Paul Raftery / View Pictures; p 79 © London Borough of Barking and Dagenham; p 80 © Peter Mackinven / View Pictures; p 81 © Edwin Jones; p 83 © Walthamstow Forest Council; p 84 © Clive Nichols/BMA House; p 86 © Mikael Schilling; p 87 © Jo Reid & John Peck; p 88 & 89 © Royal College of Physicians; p 90 & 91 © Peter Mackinven / View Pictures

LONDON AT HOME

p 92 (from top to bottom): all © Simon Upton except for second from bottom © Tim Soar; p 94 & 95 © Simon Upton; p 96 & 97 © Bexley Heritage Trust; p 98 & 99 © Simon Upton; p 100 & 101 © Marcus Lyon; p 102 & 103 © Simon Upton; p 104 © First Base; p 104–105 © Richard Brine; p 106 © Ioana Marinescu; p 107 © Tim Crocker; p 108 © Hanne Lund; p 109 © Anthony Coleman; p 110 & 111 © James Davies; p 112 & 113 © Ed Reeve; p 114 & 115 © Simon Upton; p 117, 118–119 © Helene Binet; p 120 & 121 (top) © Morley von Sternberg; p 121 (bottom) © Tim Soar; p 122 & 123 © Ivor Berresford; p 124 © Meyer Studio; p 126 & 127 © Paul Riddle; p 128 & 129 © Dr Simon Joseph; p 130 © Dr James Strike; p 131 © Kilian O'Sullivan

COMMUNITY, LEARNING AND STUDIOS

p 132 (from top to bottom): all © Simon Upton except for second from bottom © Tim Soar/ Allford Hall Monaghan Morris; p 134 © Simon Upton; p 135 © Nick Kane; p 136 & 137 © Simon Upton; p 138 © BAPS Swaminarayan Sanstha, UK; p 139 © Bevis Marks Synagogue; p 140 © Nathan Willock / View Pictures; p 141 © Paul Tolenaar; p 143 © Simon Upton; p 144 © Edmund Sumner / View Pictures; p 145 © Simon Upton; p 146 (top) Peter Cook; p 147 (bottom) & 148 © Simon Upton; p 148 & p 149 (top) © Dennis Gilbert; p 149 (bottom) © Jerwood Space; p 150 & 151 © Luke Hayes / View Pictures; p 152 & 153 © Tim Soar / Allford Hall Monaghan Morris; p 155 © Simon Upton; p 156–157 © Simon Upton; p 158 © Paul Tyagi / View Pictures; p 159 © Morley von Sternberg; p 160 & 161 © Tim Soar; p 162 © Grant Smith / View Pictures; p 163 © Richard Brine / View Pictures; p 164 & 165 © Kilian O'Sullivan / View Pictures; 166 & 167 © Simon Upton; p 168 & 169 © John Sturrock; p 170 & 171 © Tim Soar; p 172 © Paul Riddle / View Pictures; p 172–173 © University of London; p 174 © Jonny Donovan; p 176 © Jonas Lencer / dRMM; p 178 & 179 David Grandorge; p 180–181 © Simon Upton; p 182 & 183 © Richard Glover / View Pictures

CULTURE AND RECREATION

p 184 (from top to bottom): © Edmund Sumner; © Simon Upton; © Morley von Sternberg; © James Mortimer/The Interior Archive; p 186 © Grant Smith / View Pictures; p 187 © Simon Upton; p 188 © Simon Upton; p 189 © Peter Cook; p 190 & 191 Morley von Sternberg; p 192 © Simon Upton & p 193 (top); p 193 (bottom) © Hanne Lund; p 194 & 195 © Simon Upton; p 196 © Peter Cook / View Pictures; p 197 © Hufton + Crow / View Pictures; p 198 & 199 © Anthony Weller / LTA; p 200–201 & 202–203 Olympic Delivery Authority; p 204 © Adrian Mott; p 205 © Simon Upton; p 206 © Simon Upton; p 207 © Fritz von der Schulenburg / The Interior Archive; p 208 © Dylan Thomas; p 209 © Edmund Sumner; p 211 © Simon Upton; p 212 & 213 © James Mortimer/The Interior Archive